A Reasonable Person

Walter Davis

authorHOUSE®

AuthorHouse™
1663 Liberty Drive
Bloomington, IN 47403
www.authorhouse.com
Phone: 1-800-839-8640

© 2010 Walter Davis. All rights reserved.

No part of this book may be reproduced, stored in a retrieval system, or transmitted by any means without the written permission of the author.

First published by AuthorHouse 5/10/2010

ISBN: 978-1-4520-0558-4 (e)
ISBN: 978-1-4520-0557-7 (sc)
ISBN: 978-1-4520-0556-0 (hc)

Library of Congress Control Number: 2010904283

Printed in the United States of America
Bloomington, Indiana

This book is printed on acid-free paper.

To my wife, who has not only filled my life with love, but is the most reasonable person I've ever known.

Negligence is the omission to do something which a reasonable man, guided upon those considerations which ordinarily regulate the conduct of human affairs, would do, or doing something which a prudent and reasonable man would not do.

                                         Blyth v. Birmingham Water Works(1857)

ACKNOWLEDGMENTS

My main thanks have to go to 'Editing With Panacahe' which, in their editorial duties, treated my book as one of their own. Without their help and encouragement I could never have completed this project and I am deeply grateful to them for the hard work and long hours they spent with me.

Naturally I wish to thank my wife and family for their support, patience and input. They are all deeply appreciated.

Finally, I want to thank all of the judges and lawyers of the State of Hawaii. Some of you may think you recognize yourselves. However, you are wrong! All of the characters in my book are fictional. But, without all of the hard working and competent members of the Hawaiian Bar Association this book would not have been possible.

PROLOGUE

On a typical day twenty-five to thirty motor vehicle accidents will occur in the State of Hawaii. Most will be fender benders but there will be at least five or six serious injuries and a better than fifty percent chance of one death. Many will sue for whiplash type injuries.

Not only are there auto accidents but each day dozens of people are hurt in their homes, hotels or stores. They fall or things fall on them. They are burned, electrocuted, bumped, battered, bruised and broken. Under Hawaii's no fault law auto accident victims receive a minimal amount of disability payments for a limited amount of time. If they're injured on the job they get partial reimbursement by way of worker compensation payments. But others may be off work for long periods of time with no compensation, creating a significant hardship on themselves, their families and their communities.

Many of these people will file lawsuits. And this is where I come in. I'm a trial lawyer, and I'm hired by insurance companies to defend suits brought by accident victims. It's my job, using all of my skills as a trial lawyer, to convince juries to either award nothing or as little as reasonably possible. For the past twenty years, my life has been spent in preparing and trying lawsuits. It may not be the most stressful job in the world, compared with riding a bicycle on a tight wire hung between the rooftops of two skyscrapers, but I'm certain it ranks among the top ten. As a result, there are times when we may not act as reasonable people should act. I'm forty-six and feel every year of it.

The system itself ages you, putting up with its flaws, its drastic need of change, a system that has turned into one big game played in arenas called courtrooms. There are too many people who are seriously injured that receive very little, if any, compensation. On the other hand, it is gratifying to see the frauds, liars and phonies walk away with nothing..

But sometimes differentiating between the deserving and undeserving is not easy. As every lawyer knows, there's no such thing as certainty in a courtroom. Certainty is for engineers building bridges. Certainty is for doctors, who have to diagnose the nature of an illness. Certainty is for probate lawyers, who must see that the precise terms of a bequest are carried out. The most to hope for is that a judge or jury tries to reach a just decision. But there has yet to be a lie detector invented that can accurately reveal whether a person is lying or telling the truth. It's far from an unusual event when two or more witnesses to an accident relate completely conflicting versions of what occurred.

Fortunately, I don't make the final decision. It's made by claims departments, judges and juries. I'm just a hired gun.

PART 1

HAWAII
1979

Chapter 1

"Mr. Boyle, you may now give your summation," Judge Takai announces from the bench.

It's the final day of trial and we all watch William Boyle, attorney for the plaintiff, walk to the lectern. Boyle has a reputation for being merciless in a courtroom and he has certainly lived up to that reputation during this trial. In his mid fifties with a full head of premature white hair, tall and distinguished, he's a complete gentleman outside of courtrooms, but turns into a vicious cobra the moment a trial begins.

Without any notes, Boyle reconstructs what happened so vividly that all of us in the courtroom are able to visualize it. "It happened in a little house on Maui, a one story, single wall, wooden structure owned and maintained by Maui Sugar Company, one in a row of company owned houses occupied by employees and their spouses. It's an outdated custom so when both spouses die, the house is torn down. In this particular house, Irene Sato, sixty years old, petite widow of plantation worker, Taki Sato, lived alone."

Boyle is at pains to recreate the scene, even describing the interior. "It's modest but clean, freshly painted and well maintained. The furniture is plain but comfortable and sturdy. Pictures of the Sato family decorate the walls - the Satos, their son who was killed in Vietnam and their daughter."

He wants the jurors to place themselves on the scene, and by elaborating and delaying the revelation of what is to follow he heightens tension and the shock of discovery. Even though the jurors already know what happened, their reaction will be far more intense if they are made to experience it vicariously.

"And there is Irene, preparing lunch for herself and her daughter when she hears the knock on the door." To make us all see her more clearly, he even describes what she's wearing. "She's sixty years old, but hasn't lost her youthful figure, can still wear shorts and a navy blue tee shirt. Hearing the knock on the door, she's hoping it's the plumber she asked for. As she opens the door she sees a man with a tool box. He's an ordinary looking young fellow, tall and lanky, wearing khaki pants and a shirt with the words 'Maui Sugar' embroidered above the left breast pocket. This reassures her, but more reassuring is the Marine emblem tattooed on his left arm with the words 'Semper Fi' under it. Her fallen son had been a Marine."

'Hello, are you the plumber?' She asks.

'Yes ma'am,' he replies. 'I was sent over by my supervisor, Bob Lacey, to fix your commode.' He lifts the tool box."

"She smiles, opens the door and gestures for him to enter. 'I know Bob,' she says. 'I'll show you the bathroom.' Leading the way down a narrow hallway, she points out the bathroom and leaves him there, returning to the kitchen to finish preparing lunch."

"She's slicing tomatoes for sandwiches when she hears a sound behind her. Before she can turn she feels a strong arm squeeze her neck and a sharp object pressed between her shoulder blades. She drops her knife, gasping for breath. A voice whispers in her ear, "I've got a knife. Drop your shorts." She obeys and is easily forced to the floor.

"He tightens his grip on her neck and the kitchen turns into one big blur and rapidly turns dark. She can feel her panties being torn off. The last sensation she feels before she dies is being penetrated."

By now the jury is fixated on the horror of what happened. By pitching to their imaginations and creating immediacy, Boyle has virtually made them eyewitnesses to the crime, and he obviously hopes to focus their revulsion onto my client, who has employed the murderer.

"Objection!" I almost shout the words as I rise. "All of this is mere speculation on the part of counsel."

Judge Takai looks annoyed as he says, "Objection overruled, please be seated Mr. Dorsey." I sit.

Boyle, unperturbed, continues. "This 'plumber,' who had been working for Maui Sugar for a mere three days, had a dishonorable discharge from the marines for acts of violence and a police record for rape and assault with a deadly weapon. We've proven, ladies and gentlemen, by a preponderance of the evidence, not only was the defendant negligent, it was guilty of gross negligence in its hiring practices."

Again, I rise. "Objection, Your Honor. There's never been any allegation of gross negligence."

Judge Takai looks at me and almost sneers, "Objection overruled. Please continue Mr. Boyle." Again, I sit. So far I have a perfect record with this judge. He's overruled every one of my objections and sustained all of Boyle's. Once again, I thank God for juries.

Boyle continues. "As I was saying before I was so rudely interrupted, the defendant was grossly negligent causing my client indescribable mental distress. Imagine walking into her mothers home for lunch and seeing her nude body, raped and strangled by an employee who had a record of violence a mile long. You should bring back an award in the millions. Thank you."

Since when, I ask myself, *is it considered rude to object?* I try to remember why I've been taking crap like that from Boyle for the past eight days without a retort. It's certainly not because he's considered the most renowned and high powered plaintiffs attorney in the state. That never stopped me before. Oh yes, I remember, it's because this is his last trial. He's been appointed to the federal bench and who knows how many times in the future I'll have to appear before him.

Judge Takai motions for me to start my summation. I stand and walk to the podium. "Ladies and gentlemen," I begin," Eight days ago you each promised to follow the instructions which will be given to you by the court. Soon you will have to keep that promise." I remind them that the plaintiff has the burden of proof, that they are to use their common sense and that they are to decide the case without sympathy for or bias against either side. I agree that this was a terrible tragedy and that no one could feel worse about it than my client, Maui Sugar Company.

Looking at the jury, I like what I see. Six men, four of whom retired to Maui and two utility workers. An equal number of women, three housewives and three school teachers. They don't look like people who will award millions of dollars.

"Ladies and gentlemen," I continue, "We can all feel the horror that the plaintiff must have felt when she entered the house and saw her mother lying on the kitchen floor. But by no stretch of the imagination should this be blamed on Maui Sugar. All of the testimony during the past eight days has clearly shown that Maui Sugar completely followed the law in its hiring practices. And, the law is clear that it was not legally allowed to check out the criminal or military record of any prospective employee, especially such a low level maintenance worker as Roger Schmidt."

"When you're in the jury room," I tell them, "please review the rules and regulations forbidding companies to obtain any records having to do with the criminal or military background of prospective employees." I then review the testimony of the human resource people and the expert witnesses, all of whom confirmed that Maui Sugar was prohibited by law from looking at such records. "It's true," I say, "that Schmidt had a record of violence, but it's also true that there was no legal way that my client could discover that record."

What I don't mention, and what even Boyle seemed to overlook, is that Schmidt's supervisor should never have allowed the bastard to enter the woman's home by himself. After all, Schmidt had only been on the job for a few days and nothing was known about him. Certainly the supervisor did not act as a reasonable person. As I scan the members of the jury it crosses my mind that they seem too intelligent to overlook this fact. In a way, that pleases me. Even though it's my job to argue against her, I certainly empathize with the daughter and hope she receives a fair award.

In my concluding remarks, I tell them that my client acted as a reasonable employer would act under the same or similar circumstances and that they should find in favor of Maui Sugar. "However," I further tell them, "if you don't agree with me on that, the award should be no more than $50,000." Of course, what I don't tell them is that we offered $150,000 to settle which was turned down cold by Boyle. I thank them for being attentive and sit.

As the judge instructs the jury, my mind wanders. Today is Wednesday, the eighth and final day of trial. As soon as the judge finishes, I'll return to my office in Honolulu and try to catch up with some neglected paper work. Tonight it's a red eye to Denver for medical depositions in an upcoming trial, and then to San Francisco for another deposition on Friday morning. Finishing the week, I'll spend Friday afternoon with Elaine. Its been months since I've seen her and the thought of our being together, even for one afternoon, both excites me and makes me feel guilty as hell. I'm married to a wonderful, caring woman and no one appreciates her more than I do. But I've been obsessed with Elaine since we were kids, and I seem to have no control over my feelings for her. I wonder to myself, when did love become more complicated than law?

Chapter 2

I've always been an early riser. Even as a kid, during the hot Iowa summers, I'd be the first to get up, have a quick bowl of cereal, grab my baseball glove and wake my friends by banging on their windows as the sun was barely lighting up the sky. I love early mornings when the air is still cool and fresh and my mind seems clear and focused. It's a habit that remained with me through college and law school and has continued to the present.

On mornings when I'm in trial I get up even earlier than usual, which explains why I'm sitting on my lanai on this Monday morning, watching the sky turn brighter as the sun slowly lights up the ocean inching its way across my lawn and finally casts its glare directly into my eyes. The weather bureau was right. This is one of the hottest summers Honolulu has ever experienced.

Putting down the paper, I gaze at the ocean as I finish my second cup of coffee. My thoughts center on Elaine and I savor the few hours we spent together on Friday. Completing my deposition by noon, we met in the lobby of my hotel and went directly to my room. Several months had passed since our last meeting and, without saying a word, we undressed and fell on the bed. The day would have been perfect except for the feelings of guilt washing over me, except for that small inner voice telling me that this was all wrong.

As I watch some shorebirds flirting on the sand, I hear my wife's voice call out from the kitchen, "Do you want another cup?"

"No, but I would like a banana."

She comes out carrying a hot cup of coffee in one hand and two bananas in the other, wearing a flowered flannel robe with nothing underneath. As usual she's barefooted. Like many of the local people she has a mixed heritage, German and Irish with some Chinese and Hawaiian. Her features are almost perfect with high cheek bones, full lips and large brown eyes, sparkling with wit and curiosity. Her light brown complexion, jet black hair and slender, graceful figure makes her look years younger than her age of forty-two.

She takes a sip of her coffee and says, "I've hardly seen you since last weekend. You were only home for a few hours before leaving for Denver, and yesterday you were busy all day preparing for today's trial."

You're right, I'm sorry." I reply. I feel so bad that I can hardly look her in the eye. I hate myself when I lie to her.

"I understand," she says, "but I missed you, and you never told me how the Maui case turned out."

Thankful that she's changed the subject, I reply, "Maui turned out great. The jury awarded $50,000." The best thing about that was sticking it to Boyle after he had been sticking it to me for eight days.

"What's today's trial about," she asks.

"The one today is fairly simple," I say. "An aged alcoholic lawyer had too much to drink at the Queen Kapiolani Hotel. He started hitting on a couple of tourists, and when they complained he called them some nasty names. The bartender called security which had the police remove him from the premises. While this was going on, his wife was upstairs competing in a bridge tournament."

"He sounds like a real jerk. What's he suing for?"

"Assault and battery, false imprisonment and mental distress," I reply. "It shouldn't take more than two days."

"It does sound sort of silly. What time does it start?" She asks.

"Eight thirty," I reply. "The problem is the old guy is representing himself and that always makes thing more difficult." I then ask, "Is my tie all right?"

She looks at me and smiles. "Yes, it looks fine. I really like seeing you in a suit, it gives you a very handsome look."

I laugh out loud at that one. I certainly have never considered myself handsome. Even my mother never called me handsome. My features are somewhat too sharp, my nose a shade too conspicuous, my jaw a trifle too square. But I do feel that I have a somewhat imposing presence. I'm a bit over six feet and people have told me that I have the most penetrating eyes they've ever seen. And I'm hard pressed to explain my ability to discern instinctively whether a witness is telling the truth or not.

A Reasonable Person

Finishing my coffee, I look towards the ocean and see the same three fishermen that are out there almost every morning, squatting on the beach, their lines floating on top of the water. I can hear their muffled laughter as they sit talking and, as usual, not paying any attention whatsoever to their fishing lines. These three old guys just enjoy having some time together on the beach.

I'm hoping that someday I'll have time to loaf for hours, sitting on the beach, trading stories with my buddies, my fishing line suspended in the water. But chances are I'll have a heart attack or a stroke long before that happens.

For now, it's an idle daydream, imagining how it would be to live a life without the stress or pressure that fill my days.

As Kathy sips her coffee, we sit quietly enjoying the changing colors of the ocean, the stillness of the morning, the singing of the birds and the occasional sound of the laughter coming from the men on the beach.

I look at her and feel as attracted to her now as I did eleven years ago when we were first married. Her first, my second, everything a man could want in a wife – devoted, intelligent, attractive, the proverbial good wife whose worth is far beyond red coral. Why would any man want more?

Kathy asks, "Is there anything interesting in the paper?"

I hand her the newspaper. She can tell that my mind is somewhere else even as I answer, "I didn't see anything of interest Oh yes, we haven't had a hotter August in Honolulu since the weather bureau started keeping statistics. And here I am wearing a tie."

She smiles and begins to tease me. "I'm sure glad I don't have to get all dressed up today. I think I'll lounge by the pool or on the lawn this morning while you're earning a living for us in that sweltering courtroom."

I get up and move over to kiss her goodbye. "It sure pays to have a cushy job with the Board of Education. I wish I could have the summer off."

"You'd go nuts if you took off for a summer. Don't forget," she adds, "We're meeting at the Oahu Country Club at seven tonight. It's Lynn's birthday and I'm taking her out for golf this afternoon." Lynn Cooper, an attractive thirty-five year old former para-legal, is my partner's wife.

I give her a kiss goodbye and tell her, "I'm looking forward to it, I'll see you tonight."

I pull out of my driveway and since it's early head for the freeway. Most of the houses on Kahala Beach are large and expensive, they're mainly stately old homes protected by large fences and stone walls. Long driveways wind through yards landscaped with exotic plants, swimming pools and even some tennis courts. Ours is one of the smaller and less expensive homes but there's nowhere else I'd rather live.

"Oh shit!" I yell out as I pull onto the freeway. Not even seven and traffic has come to a virtual standstill. As I inch forward I see the reason. A three-car accident is completely blocking the fast lane. I slowly approach the accident scene and can finally see the lanes opening up in front of me.

As I pass the wreckage, I see three men waving their hands at each other. Thankfully, there don't seem to be any serious injuries. Smiling inwardly, I think, if there were injuries, the victims would be holding the business cards of at least a half-dozen lawyers. Of course, within a few weeks they may all be claiming whiplash type injuries and end up suing each other. I recall the last whiplash case I handled. Our investigator had movies of the plaintiff carrying a huge transmission. I settled that one cheap.

Regardless of what Kathy may think, I'd love to take off for a summer, maybe even a year or two. But this is no time to make any drastic decisions. Not with two kids in college, large house payments and a trial schedule that seems to go on forever. Maybe in a year or two things will be different and I can escape the whims of judges and juries. Perhaps, in time, some of our associates will be able to take over some of the trial load. The alternative is too depressing to contemplate.

Despite the traffic jam it takes only twenty minutes to reach the parking garage of my downtown office building. Entering the bakery on the ground floor, I inhale the aroma of freshly baked bread. Standing behind the counter is Freida, the owner, a transplant from Germany. Freida is in her early sixties, rather plump but pretty for her age with great breasts trying to break out of her too tight top. I ask for my usual bran muffin and ask, "Did you have a wild weekend?"

She laughs as she wraps my muffin, "All of my weekends are wild." I smile to myself wondering what it would be like to have a wild weekend with Freida. I take the elevator to the twentieth floor and enter the koa wood doors with the small bronze sign, "Dorsey & Cooper, Attorneys at Law."

I'm the Dorsey. Mark Dorsey. My partner is Frank Cooper. We have six associates, two paralegals, five legal secretaries, an office manager, two bookkeepers, a receptionist, file clerk and a messenger. As usual, I'm the first one in the office.

Even though bright outside, it's so dark inside I have trouble finding the light switch. Standing in the dark, I think of the loads of paperwork and my seemingly unending trial schedule. It seems overwhelming, and I remind myself that it's all part of the workload taken on when running a successful firm. Still, my mood is as dark as the room, and it's not about my workload. It's knowing I won't see Elaine again for several months. Again I ask myself, why would a man want more than a wife like Kathy? Why indeed, I tell myself as I turn on the lights and walk to my office to complete preparing my opening statement for today's trial.

CHAPTER 3

As I return from court, Marsha looks at her watch. It's already ten after twelve, and the receptionist hands her a brown paper bag, which she carries into the coffee room. There she takes out a turkey sandwich and a pickle and places them on a paper plate. Then she pours fresh coffee into a cup, and hurries into my office to place the plate and cup on my desk as I step into the room. I quickly slip off my jacket and drape it over the back of my desk chair. Reaching for the sandwich, I inhale a huge bite and wash it down with a sip of the steaming coffee. I look at the stacks of paper sitting in front of me and stifle a huge groan. I can't believe all of this came in since I left for court this morning. It feels like being buried under mounds of paper. I have less than an hour to try to dispose of as much as I can before returning for the afternoon session.

"How is the case going?" Marsha asks me. "Fast," I reply through a mouthful of pickle. "We've selected the jury and made opening statements. Greig will testify this afternoon. Tomorrow morning will be the hotel people. We'll settle instructions and argue tomorrow afternoon. A very quick trial."

"And also one of the silliest," she mutters, as she leaves the room. She's absolutely right, I think to myself. This is one of the most inane cases I've tried in a long time. I gobble down the rest of my sandwich and gaze out the window at the ever expanding city of Honolulu. The view never fails to impress me. In the background is Diamond Head flanked by a jade green ocean and clear blue skies marred only by the incredible number of yellow construction cranes. By now, the yellow crane has been dubbed the new state bird.

A Reasonable Person

I look again at the mass of papers on my desk. Marsha has put them in three neat piles consisting of correspondence, pleadings and new cases. She won't let me see what she classifies as junk mail until my trial is over.

I call Marsha back, and she stands next to me as I look through the pleadings, which consist mainly of discovery items in pending cases to be reviewed by one of my paralegals or associates. I hand these to Marsha with instructions as to whom each document should be assigned.

There are also answers to interrogatories and documents in a number of cases received in response to requests for production. I set these aside as they'll have to be reviewed more carefully at the end of the day. These responses constitute the springboard from which I can then start the preparation of my cases. From them I obtain the information necessary to subpoena medical and employment records, obtain witness statements, schedule depositions, determine whether it's necessary to obtain expert witnesses and start the innumerable other tasks essential in preparing a case for trial.

Then I start on my correspondence. After scanning each letter I hand them to Marsha with instructions on how to handle them. Those that require personal responses I put in a separate pile. Although Marsha has been working as a legal secretary for twenty years and for me for more than seven, she remarks that she's constantly amazed at the speed with which I read the letters and the quick decisions I make regarding each one. I refrain from telling her that if I had time to think I would be too overwhelmed to make any decisions.

Looking at the last pile, I ask, "How many new cases came in?"

"Three, but I've already received extensions to answer so there should be no problems. All of the lawyers are cooperative. You won't have to worry about them until your trial is over. You look tired. Would you like another cup of coffee before going back?"

She can read my mind. "Yes. Thanks."

I watch her as she leaves the room. In her early fifties, she's tall and still slender with graying hair, which she's now beginning to tint. Not especially pretty but always well groomed, she has an attractive appearance. Once again, I realize how lucky I am to have her as my secretary. She is by far the best I've ever had. Although every trial lawyer in town is constantly trying to hire her away she is completely loyal to me. More importantly, no one will match the salary I'm paying her.

I look at my watch and see that I must leave in twenty minutes. I go through my telephone messages. Nothing earth shattering. Some claims adjusters probably wanting to discuss the status of their cases and a few calls from plaintiffs' attorneys wanting to settle cases. I can return the calls after the trial is over. Marsha returns with the coffee and places it in front of me. As I take a sip she says with affected disinterest, "You had a collect call from San Rafael, California. Someone named Elaine. She wouldn't leave a number. She said she'd call back."

She's watching me closely for a reaction, but after twenty years of jury trials keeping a blank expression is easy. I give no outward sign that my spirits have risen immeasurably. I continue sipping my coffee and keep a mildly curious look as I ask, "Did she say what company she's with or who she is?"

"No. It sounded more like a personal call. She wouldn't give any information at all." Marsha is staring at me as if trying to read my mind and half believing that she can succeed.

I know she would kill to know who Elaine is so I put on what I hope is a thoughtful but unconcerned expression, "She doesn't sound too familiar to me. Could be an old client who has a problem."

"She didn't sound too old to me."

Fortunately, before the conversation goes any further, Frank Cooper barges in and sprawls on my couch. Marsha is obviously not happy with the interruption, but since Frank is my partner she gets up to leave, sharply reminding me that I only have ten more minutes.

Frank makes an obscene gesture to her back as she walks out. "What's wrong with her today? Usually she's pretty friendly."

"She was trying to pump me for what she thought was some juicy gossip."

"She does love gossip. She looked like she was ready to bite my head off. How's the trial going?"

"Fast. We've selected the jury and given opening statements. Greig will testify this afternoon. Tomorrow morning we'll put on the hotel people and the cop. We should argue in the afternoon."

Frank looks surprised, "That is fast. How does the jury look?"

"Typical," I reply. "I wanted twelve women bridge players. We only have five and we wouldn't have them if Greig hadn't helped."

"What do you mean," Frank asks.

"I know it sounds unbelievable but Greig also wanted women bridge players."

Frank looks skeptical. "It seems to me he wouldn't want either women or bridge players. Neither would have much sympathy for what he was doing in the bar."

"Very true," I say. "I don't understand it either."

"What do you think will be the outcome?"

"I think it should be a defense verdict. The hotel people had every right to trespass him. Besides, he admitted in his opening statement that they never touched him so how can it be assault and battery? That's the most dangerous charge. By the way do you know Greig?"

"Not personally, but I've heard of him. Apparently at one time he was considered a competent attorney, but he started drinking and the last ten years have been all downhill for him. He has one or two clients left who keep him on a small retainer. Probably more out of pity than for any other reason."

This bit of news saddens me. "I hope we don't end up like that. It's too bad, but he was really out of it at the hotel. He was screaming like a madman when they took his picture and when the police officer escorted him off the premises he kept calling the officer a fucking pig."

Frank grins, "I can't believe he's actually going to trial. I'd love to watch him testify but I've got two depositions this afternoon. I start trial on Wednesday."

I look out my window and observe a 747 slowly climbing towards the east. I watch it ascend until it climbs out of view and then say a little caustically, "This is only Monday. Why not hold off until tomorrow?"

Frank starts laughing, "You know me. Always prepared."

I get up and put on my jacket. Frank and I have been partners for almost ten years and I can't recall the last time he lost a case. He's the most natural trial lawyer I've ever known. But I can't help telling him, "You're a malpractice case waiting to happen."

As I walk out the door, Frank snuggles deeper into the couch and closes his eyes thinking there's no reason why he shouldn't take a little nap before his depositions start.

CHAPTER 4

As I exit my near freezing air-conditioned office building I look at my watch. Court starts in less than fifteen minutes and Judge Park is never late. The hot air hits me like an exploding oven. It's already close to 90 degrees with staggering humidity. The sun is so hot and the air so clear that the surroundings appear harsh and severe. I cross King Street and walk the three short blocks to the Judiciary Building. Before entering I glance at the huge gold plated statue of King Kamehameha guarding the entrance. Though strongly believing that there's no substitute for being prepared I, nonetheless, follow the habit of most Honolulu trial attorneys by asking the long dead warrior-king for luck.

The courthouse is archaic, dating back to the early 20th century and showing its age. The entrance consists of a large round rotunda with a faded Hawaiian seal engraved in the floor tile. The tile itself is so worn that spots of dull gray concrete peek through. Twin stairways flank the rotunda leading to the courtroom of the Hawaii Supreme Court. The steps are made of mahogany as are the railings but the wood has deteriorated so that none of its original richness remains. The foyer retains only a specter of its former dignity. Portraits of previous Supreme Court justices cover the dull white walls. They all seem to have the same disdainful look as if every lawyer who appears before them is an incompetent idiot.

There are six circuit courtrooms on the ground level and four more on the second floor in addition to the Supreme Court and law library. The building is too old for central air and its one elevator is usually out of order so I'm pleased that Judge Parks' courtroom is on the first floor.

A Reasonable Person

As I approach the courtroom a loud voice hails me. "Mark! Wait up a second!"

I turn and see Bill Cohn hurrying in my direction flagging me down with his briefcase. Cohn is the plaintiffs' attorney in a number of cases I'm defending. He approaches with a serious look on his face. Though only in his mid-thirties, he looks ten years older. His face is well lined with wrinkles, his hair is thinning and rapidly turning gray. Also, he has all of the moral inclinations of a traffic signal. I think to myself that the general practice of law is obviously too much for Cohn. The stress is getting to him.

"Mark," Cohn gasps, "I've got to discuss the Rostky case with you." Though he's only trotted for a few yards he's already out of breath.

"Damn it, Bill, you ought to get some exercise. At this rate you'll have a heart attack by the time you're forty. I'm half

teasing but Cohn takes me seriously.

"My heart's in great shape. It's the damn ulcer that's killing me."

For the tenth time in as many minutes I check my watch. I hate being late for court. "I'm in a hurry. I can't keep Park waiting. He'll give me an ulcer. What's the Rostky case about?"

Cohn's right eye is twitching and he pulls nervously at his tie, a habit that annoys everyone who tries to carry on a conversation with him. "You remember. A couple of thugs beat him up with cue sticks at some cocktail lounge. You represent the bar."

I vaguely recall the case. According to the manager, Rostky was a frequent customer who enjoyed playing pool, drinking beer and generally acting obnoxious. One evening he got a little too offensive and two young customers beat on him with their cue sticks. The manager called the police and tried to break up the fight but not before poor Rostky had been knocked unconscious. The assailants also gave the manager a few blows and then ran out. They never were caught. "Bill, I'm really in a hurry. What's the problem?"

Cohn's left eye starts twitching, "I want to settle the case. If we do it quickly we can settle it cheap."

It's obvious something drastic has happened. Normally Cohn doesn't settle cheap until the day of trial. I definitely have to check this out. I say to him, "Let's talk about it later. I'll give you a call after I finish my trial."

I enter the courtroom and see that all but the judge are in their appointed positions. The jury is seated, as are the court clerk and court reporter. The law clerk, a recent law school graduate, is standing behind the judge's chair looking at some papers. He's the only one in the courtroom, other than Greig and me, wearing a coat and tie. Greig is sitting on his side of the long counsel table and Sammy Auwai, the hotel manager, is seated on my side.

I plop down, open my file, take out my pen and glance at the jury. Twelve of the usual suspects. Several housewives, two telephone company employees, a school teacher and a few retirees. My plan, during jury selection, was to keep as many bridge players and women on the jury as possible even if it meant using all of my peremptory challenges to do so. To my surprise, Greig, contrary to his own self interest, also wanted bridge players and women on the jury. As a result, we have seven women and five men. Five of the jurors are bridge players.

In Hawaii, it takes ten of the twelve jurors to agree in order to reach a verdict. Watching them interact, it's clear they've already broken down into little cliques. That's good. I dislike juries when the members don't get along, I never know what one or two might do out of spite.

Sammy leans over and whispers in my ear, "Look at Greig. I think he's half tanked. I could swear I smelled alcohol when I walked by him."

I look over. Sure enough, his complexion is flushed and his eyes, behind thick horn rimmed glasses, look bloodshot. Even his balding scalp looks ruddier than it did before lunch. He's not very tall so his paunch makes him look almost pregnant. I tell Sammy, "I think you're right but I hope not. Park could call a mistrial."

While waiting for the judge, I focus on the courtroom. It's huge with large windows to my left and the jury box on my right. The wooden ceiling is at least twenty feet high giving the room the acoustics of a discotheque. The judge's bench looms like a throne above the court, enabling him to look down on us as if he were King Kamehameha presiding over his subjects. The room is kept no more than ten degrees cooler than the outside temperature by means of noisy air conditioners fastened to the windows. Between the disco-like acoustics and the blaring air conditioners, you have to practically yell to be heard. The loudspeaker system does little to help. If the air conditioners malfunction, the windows are opened and the traffic sounds become deafening.

But, strangely, I love it. I think it beats the modern courthouses all to hell. The State is soon going to start construction of a contemporary courthouse and I dread the thought. This has a sense of history, an aura of real justice being handed out, an atmosphere where legal precedent is truly meaningful. Of equal importance, I think to myself, is the fact that there's too much noise for any of the jurors to fall asleep.

At exactly half past the hour the door leading from chambers opens and Judge Gordon Y. B. Park steps onto the platform. Before the bailiff can utter the words commanding everyone to stand, all of the people in the courtroom jump to their feet. Most of the jurors refuse to look directly at the judge perhaps thinking that such an act, if not illegal, is certainly sacrilegious.

The law clerk, who also doubles as bailiff, yells out at the top of his lungs, "All rise!"

Since everyone in the room is already standing, there's complete silence, as if nobody knows what to do next. Even the judge looks somewhat undecided, but Park being indecisive is not exactly a novel event.

Judge Park is the first Korean lawyer in the State of Hawaii, if not the United States, to be appointed to the bench. Y.B. had never been a particularly talented lawyer. He's slow thinking and deliberate but has the tenacity of a bulldog. He got this job when political pressures, which are often driven by race in Hawaii, forced the governor to appoint a Korean to the circuit court. Park gets hold of a new, at least to him, legal concept, chews on it, struggles with it and makes you repeatedly explain it and show him how it applies to the facts of the case in front of him until he finally understands it.

However, this is not what bothers most of the lawyers who appear in front of him. His real problem is that he has the judicial temperament of a serial killer. Sometimes it seems as if the slightest suggestion that he might be wrong sends him into a frenzy. A year ago, Frank had myself and two of our associates near hysteria telling us about his trial against Howard Kim in Park's courtroom.

"After the jury was dismissed, following the second day of trial," Frank told us, "The two Koreans got into an argument over a legal issue. Within minutes they were yelling at each other, and I thought the Korean War was starting up again. Park held Howard in contempt and fined him one hundred dollar. Howard told Park that he didn't have any cash on him so Park told the bailiff to take poor Howard to the lock up area until the fine was paid. Since I didn't have enough cash I had to call Howard's office to bring the money."

"Since then," Frank added, "I'm never without a hundred bucks in Park's courtroom." Neither am I.

The law clerk's shout is easily heard over the noise of the window conditioners, "Please be seated!"

Following the judge's lead everyone sits. Judge Park inspects the courtroom and, looking like he's going to swallow the microphone says, "May the record please show that all members of the jury are present along with the plaintiff who is representing himself and the defendants' representative and its counsel. Good afternoon ladies and gentlemen, we will proceed. Mr. Greig, you may call your first witness."

CHAPTER 5

Leaving the courthouse, I pick up my car and drive to the Chinatown district of downtown Honolulu. Geographically it's close to my office, but a world away with its wide variety of unique delicacies ranging from pigs feet to seaweed and salmon heads. The Chinese seem to be adept at concocting delicious dishes from almost anything. I stop at a small flower shop and in case Frank forgot that it's her birthday, I buy a ginger lei for Lynn. The sweet aroma of honeysuckle fills the room, reminding me of the open fields of Iowa. I also buy one for Kathy, more modest, but helping to assuage the guilt of my preoccupation with Elaine.

The trial is going well but that's certainly no reason to celebrate. Greig is a pitiable opponent, and defeating him will give me little satisfaction.

I enter the cocktail lounge of the Oahu Country Club trying to forget the stack of paper work I left on my desk. As I walk through the already crowded cocktail lounge, I wave hello to a number of acquaintances. Oahu is the oldest and most staid country club in Honolulu, but its members are completely diversified, making it a microcosm of the melting pot where we live. Caucasians are definitely in the minority, making it very different from the clubs I've visited on the mainland.

I spy Frank, sitting at a table, nursing a mai-tai, staring out the window. An inexpensive plumeria lei is sitting on the table in front of him, probably the least celebratory of leis. I walk over to join him and order a vodka tonic. We're comfortable in our surroundings and with each other. Those who are superficially acquainted with us are surprised that we've remained partners for so long. In demeanor, as in physical appearance, we have very little in common. While I'm tall, slender and clean shaven, Frank is short and somewhat chubby but strikingly handsome with a bushy mustache, blue eyes as clear as rainwater and thick black hair that has never been cut by anyone but the most expensive stylists since his days as a naval aviator.

His eyes are his most striking feature. Most people make the mistake of looking at his smiling mouth and the cheerful crinkling around his eyes receiving the impression that he's a happy go lucky type of person. They couldn't be more wrong. They don't look deep into his blue diamond eyes, so never see the coldness which lurks there, mirroring the reality that this is no dolphin but a true piranha waiting to tear the flesh from any unsuspecting lawyer who comes across him in a courtroom. He's an antagonist of unparalleled ferocity.

But the differences between us go beyond the mere physical. Frank is the extrovert- gregarious, outgoing, seemingly never worried about any of his cases until the day of trial. On the surface, what borders on a lack of concern may seem like an impressive characteristic, but I've put enough time in courtrooms to know that someday he's liable to pay for his nonchalance.

On the other hand, my own habits and tendencies are just the opposite. I take all of my cases seriously and am obsessive about seeing that they're all properly prepared well in advance of their trial date. I try to anticipate all possible contingencies.

It isn't that Frank doesn't prepare. He always does, but typically he waits until the last minute, assuming that since the vast majority of cases settle, there's no reason to sweat it until you have to. Perhaps it's due to his experiences as a navy pilot. He told me that the flying part was easy and the only time he had to sweat it was when making a carrier landing. Nonetheless, his attitude of continually putting things off scares the hell out of me.

In a courtroom, Frank is the archetypal TV trial lawyer - flamboyant, dramatic, with a natural flair for entertaining that enables him to charm even as he dazzles with his near genius intellect and applies his technical background in mechanical engineering.

My courtroom style is very different-straightforward, reserved, almost professorial , a more scholarly approach. My inclination is to want jurors to feel they're being instructed, not entertained.

The main reason we've stayed together as partners for the past ten years is that we're both good in court and since Frank has no aptitude for running the business side of the law firm he's delighted to leave that up

A Reasonable Person

to me. Also, and almost equally important, we each have a good sense of humor and genuinely like each other.

We're sitting in front of an enormous picture window providing us with a view overlooking three lush fairways, downtown Honolulu, the Aloha Tower, two large cruise ships tied to their docks and beyond to a small flotilla of sailboats lazily cruising in front of the setting sun. The sun, dark red against an almost colorless sky, seems only inches above the horizon as it sinks like an elevator into the ocean. I nurse my vodka tonic while Frank is sipping his mai-tai.

The panoramic scene hypnotizes us. Once the sun disappears I turn to Frank, "I don't think I'll ever get tired of this view."

"Me either. I love it up here. How did your trial go?"

"Unbelievable. At first I felt sorry for the old guy. After all, he's paid his dues as far as the practice of law is concerned."

"By the time he finished testifying," I continue, "he didn't appear very sympathetic and came across as an offensive nitwit. I find it hard to believe that the jury will have much empathy for him."

"Frank smiles, "I don't think charm was ever one of his strong points."

Sipping my drink, I say, "He testified that he came to pick up his wife who was playing in a bridge tournament at the hotel. Being early, he went into the cocktail lounge to wait for her. For no apparent reason, two women sitting next to him at the bar complained about him to the bartender. The bartender asked him to leave and when he refused, a security officer appeared. Claiming he didn't want to make a scene, he followed the guard into the hotel lobby. Frank interrupts, "You mean he actually testified that he didn't know why they wanted him to leave?"

"That's right. On cross-examination, I asked him if he remembered calling the women ugly bitches. He said he'd never do that. I showed Greig a copy of his American Express bill clearly indicating that he had five glasses of wine, but he insisted that he only had two. Tomorrow the bartender will testify that Greig had five glasses of wine which is verified by his American Express bill. He'll further testify that Greig was refused anything more to drink and was hitting on the two women who were trying to ignore him. The bartender will also say he heard Greig call the women ugly bitches at which point he asked Greig to leave. When Greig refused, he had no choice but to call security."

Frank asks, "What about the assault and battery?"

I can't help chuckling and reply, "I asked Greig whether anyone from the hotel laid a hand on him. He frankly admitted that he was never touched nor did any employee of the hotel ever physically threaten him. I got him to repeat that three different ways."

"So," Frank says, "Even Y.B. Park has to dismiss the assault and battery charge."

"That's right, he will. But wait, there's more. Greig testified that after leaving the bar, the security officer told him he'd have to leave the hotel since he was drunk and disorderly. Greig kept repeating that he wouldn't leave the hotel and besides he was a lawyer and was going to sue the shit out of the hotel and all of its employees."

A look of disbelief crosses Franks' face. "You mean he admitted he said all of that? Do you think he had a few drinks during the noon recess?"

"It sure looked like it. He also told the security officer that by the time it was all over he would end up owning the hotel. At that point the officer took him to the security office, had him photographed, filled out a city trespass form, called the police and had him escorted off the premises by a police officer."

Frank says, "That's standard procedure, isn't it?"

"Absolutely. But, here's the good part. The officer who came happened to be a motorcycle cop. I asked Greig if it weren't true that a police officer escorted him off the premises. He emphatically denied it. I asked him if that person had a uniform, a badge, a gun, wore boots, had a cap and handcuffs. He admitted all of that but still denied the guy was a police officer."

Frank laughs, "What did he think he was, a priest?"

I smile and continue, "I asked him, 'If you didn't think he was a police officer, why did you call him a pig?' With that, Greig reared back and roared, 'I wouldn't call anyone a fucking pig!' You could literally hear a pin drop in the courtroom. The jurors looked like they were doing all they could to hold back their laughter. Even Park had to put his head down. He asked Greig if he had anything further and then recessed for the afternoon."

By now Frank is laughing so loud that club members are starting to stare. He lowers his voice. "Mark, that's great. Who will testify besides the bartender?"

"The hotel manager, security officer and then the police officer. The hotel manager will testify as to the procedures which were set up between all of the hotels and the police department for removing trespassers and other troublemakers.

Frank has no doubts about the outcome. "Park will dismiss the assault and battery counts so all you'll have left are false imprisonment and negligent infliction of emotional distress. My guess is that those will be dismissed as well and Greig will end up paying court costs."

"You're probably right about that. Y.B. called me into chambers after recessing and apologized for being so nice to the plaintiff. He told me that in every case where a party represents himself he leans over backwards for that person. I told him if I were a judge, I'd do the same thing."

"Frank says, "So would I. I hate trying cases where the other party is representing himself."

By now the sun has disappeared beneath the horizon leaving a completely different view. In the distance a multitude of lights shine from the windows of downtown office buildings. Further out are the twinkling multi-colored lights of several dinner cruise boats carrying hordes of tourists from Honolulu Harbor to Diamond Head. Hopefully, they're enjoying their buffet dinners while gazing at the lights of Waikiki from the ocean.

I ask Frank. "If you were Greig's lawyer, how would you have handled the case?"

Frank thinks for a minute. "Assuming I took the case in the first place," he replies, "I'd have Greig admit that he was intoxicated and acted inappropriately. In closing argument, I'd point out that the bartender should have stopped selling him drinks once Greig seemed like he was getting intoxicated, that the security guard could have taken him to the coffee shop and let him have coffee and sober up. I think he'd have had a better chance of winning."

"Absolutely," I agree. "I'd have submitted jury instructions stating that the hotel had a duty not to serve him drinks once he showed signs of being intoxicated. I think either one of us might have won the case."

I then continue, "Sometimes I feel we're on the wrong side, that we're wasting our talents for the wrong cause. I went to law school with the naïve belief that I'd be able to use my training and abilities to help people, that I would join legal aid or a similar organization which benefit people and the community, but here I am helping rich companies get richer."

Frank asks, "If you could do it over, what would you do?"

I smile. "I don't think it would be law. Probably teaching. I enjoy kids and I'm sure it would be much more rewarding than what we're doing now."

Frank says, "You may be right, but I think we're stuck doing what we're doing. It's like being caught in a velvet trap."

Not to change the subject," I ask, "but how are you getting along with Lynn? The last time we spoke about it you said things were going downhill."

He takes a sip of his drink and says, "Not too good. We just don't seem to get along very well." It's obvious he's holding back but I think this is neither the time nor place to delve deeper into his marital problems. "How about you and Kathy?" He asks. He probes me with his blue diamond eyes. He's clearly skeptical about relationships since his is going so badly.

I answer truthfully, "Kathy and I couldn't get along better. She's fantastic." Perhaps the warmth of my response is generated by a desire to conceal what's really on my mind, the phone call from Elaine. Frank is difficult to fool, especially since we've known each other for so long. He has a true trial lawyers instinct to sense when something is being withheld from him by a witness or a friend.

At that moment, as though summoned by our conversation about them, our wives appear, and we rise from our chairs.

Frank slips his lei over Lynn's head and gives her a kiss on the cheek. It appears as if she slightly pulls away from his display of affection. Though she smiles and thanks him, there's no warmth in her eyes. The lei goes perfectly with her purple and white sleeveless blouse which is tucked into bone white pants. Lynn is a slender, attractive platinum blonde who, in my opinion, overdoes make-up and lipstick. The fact that she's several inches taller than Frank doesn't seem to bother him. He's always liked tall women.

I place my lei on Lynn, plant a kiss on her cheek and wish her a happy birthday. She smiles. "Thank you, Mark. That's very sweet of you."

Kathy looks beautiful as usual. She's wearing navy blue pants with a sheer pink blouse and a matching cardigan sweater that brings out the softness in her complexion. I place my second lei over Kathy's head and start to kiss her on the cheek but she turns her head so our lips meet. "Thank you," she says, "but, it's not my birthday." I kiss her again and hold her chair so she can sit.

"How are you two?" Kathy smiles. "Talking about cases, I'll bet."

"I'll bet you have that right," Lynn says, "What else do lawyers have to talk about?" Frank and I smile, beckon to the waiter and order drinks. A glass of Chardonnay for Kathy, a vodka martini on the rocks for Lynn.

On the whole, it's a pleasant evening, though I can feel the tension between Frank and Lynn. I wonder how long they'll be together. Kathy regards me with a warm loving expression, the look of a woman secure in a relationship with a partner she loves. I smile back and place my hand over hers and try not to think about when I'm going to return Elaine's call.

CHAPTER 6

It's not quite seven and I'm at my desk eating a bran muffin and sipping my coffee. Having prepared my witnesses and final argument on the Greig case, I look at the new cases. There are three from the previous morning and two more were added in the afternoon. Marsha has set up new files, checked for possible conflicts and called all the attorneys involved for extensions of time to answer the complaints.

They appear to be fairly routine, three auto accidents with whiplash type injuries, a slip and fall in a local supermarket and a construction accident with minor injuries. Long ago I learned not to get emotionally involved in any of my cases, but to apply my skills to winning for my clients. Still, I can't help but wonder, once again, if I'm on the right side.

All of the complaints can be quickly answered and then turned over to associates for handling of discovery. I dictate answers to two of the complaints and instructions as to which associates should handle them. I can do the others later.

I go to the coffee room, pour myself another cup, return to my desk and read a report prepared by our office manager on comparative salaries in Honolulu law offices for non-professional employees. The report concludes that our firm is still above average. That's not surprising. I've always believed in treating employees well. I dictate a memo complimenting her on the excellent and comprehensive report. I'm pleased that salaries won't have to be reviewed for another six months.

A shrill voice blares through the intercom announcing a call on line one. Obviously one of the para-legals, since it's still too early for the receptionist. Knowing how irritating this is to most employees, I'll talk to her about trying not to scream into the telephone. I pick up the phone and answer, "Hello."

An unfamiliar male voice replies, "Hello. Is this Mark Dorsey?"

"Yes it is. Who's this?"

"My name is Paul Dixon. I'm general counsel for Chicago Industries. We were recently served with a lawsuit that was filed in the U.S. District Court for the District of Hawaii. The head of claims of General Indemnity Insurance Company referred us to you. Are you interested in taking on this case?"

Dixon sounds friendly but somewhat formal, probably because he spends most of his time sitting at his desk writing contracts. He should realize that our business is lawsuits. Turning down a case would be the same as a department store refusing to sell its merchandise. But, since Chicago Industries is one of the Fortune 500 and General Indemnity is a good client, I reply in my most polite tone, "Certainly, what's the case about?"

Dixon responds, "One of our divisions manufactures football helmets. Apparently our helmets were sold to a high school on Maui and one of the players, while making a tackle, received a very serious head injury. His brain stem was permanently damaged and he's now a quadriplegic. The claim is that we either designed or manufactured a defective helmet. What they've alleged is that the helmets are supposed to protect football players from exactly this type of injury. The boy is only sixteen."

My sixteen year old nephew comes to mind and how tragic it would be if he had to live out his life unable to move from the neck down. I utter, "How horrible! A sixteen year old quadriplegic!"

"Yeah, it's terrible. The president of our company is giving serious consideration to discontinuing the manufacture of helmets. Meanwhile, we can sure use your help on this case."

It crosses my mind that football helmets are probably not very profitable items. But, at times, I can be cynical. I take some basic information including the title of the lawsuit, the case number, the name of the plaintiff's attorney and the date of service of the complaint. My mind jumps into auto-drive and I ask, "Are you insured for this type of risk and have there been any prior cases or claims involving your helmets?"

"We're insured with General Indemnity with a $250,000 deductible which includes attorney's fees and costs so we have complete control over the case, including who we retain to defend us. You and your firm were very highly recommended. As to your second question, the answer is no.

We've had no prior claims of this nature. However, I understand there have been a number of these cases throughout the country and some companies have stopped manufacturing helmets as a result of these lawsuits."

Pausing a moment to reflect, I reply, "I don't believe we've had any of these cases yet in Hawaii. This is probably the first. By the way, are you calling from Chicago?"

"Yes. What time is it there?"

"Close to eight. How's the weather there?"

"Hot and humid. In the nineties with the humidity as high. How is it there?"

I look out my window and can almost feel the heat. "About seventy," I lie, "with no humidity and not a cloud in the sky. A nice trade wind is cooling us off." Since it's already in the high eighties with no trade winds, I think the Hawaii Visitors Bureau would be quite proud of me.

Dixon sighs, "I wish I were there. Maybe I'll have to come out personally to confer with you about the case."

I laugh, "Otherwise we probably won't be able to properly handle it. Meanwhile, why don't you express the complaint to us along with any other correspondence or documents you have on it and I'll get an extension to answer from the plaintiff's attorney. When did the accident take place?"

"About a year and a half ago. The complaint was our first notice of a potential claim."

I groan to myself and say to Dixon, "That makes things even a little more difficult. We'd better get an investigator on it right away so we can get reports from the school and start questioning all witnesses who may still be available."

"Good idea. We'll leave that to your discretion." By the way, are you familiar with the plaintiff's attorneys?"

I look at my notes. "Yes. We know them very well. They're a top notch plaintiffs' firm." I don't tell him that I try to play tennis once a week with the senior partner. Sometimes it's not easy for attorneys on the mainland to understand how close the legal fraternity is in Honolulu and, notwithstanding that, how hard we fight each other in court, like professionals on the tennis circuit. I go on, "I'm pretty well tied up myself so I may give it to Frank Cooper, my partner. He's a fine trial lawyer and has a background in mechanical engineering so is really good on these product liability cases."

"Sounds good to me, but we would appreciate your keeping a close eye on it. It obviously involves a very serious injury."

"Certainly. No problem, Paul. Send it out and we'll keep in touch. We report regularly to our clients on all cases." This is something I firmly insist on and one of the reasons our firm has such an excellent reputation.

"That's what I've heard. Thanks for handling it, Mark. I feel better already. I hope to get out there and meet you personally. Goodbye."

I say goodbye and hang up. There's a pile of correspondence on my desk. Catching up with dictation is going to take hours, and I have to prepare for a trial starting on Monday. I have no idea what that case is about. I'd love to call Elaine now, but there's no telling how long the conversation might take and I have to leave soon for court. But still, I think wistfully, maybe I can call her. I try to kid myself and imagine that a call won't take up that much of my time. Connecting with her, even briefly on the phone, will banish all the pressure, stress and distractions which plague me, and I'll be a kid again, if only for a moment.

Then I hear Marsha rustling about outside. She sticks her head in my doorway and says, "Only twenty minutes to go. Do you want another cup of coffee?"

"Yes, please. By the way, I spoke to Bill Cohn yesterday about the Rostky case. He said something about another accident and wants to settle. Pull the file and see who's working with me on it. I think it's David. Have him check with the police department to see if there's been some sort of new accident and get the report for me. You know Cohn. Sometimes he tries to be slick."

As she goes for the coffee I close my eyes and lean back in my chair. 'Shit', I say to myself, 'There just isn't enough time to do it all.'

What I'm really thinking is that I can't do what I really want to do, call Elaine. That will have to wait for another day.

CHAPTER 7

As anticipated the trial moves quickly. It's Tuesday afternoon and Greig is delivering his argument to the jury in a monotone that threatens to put the entire courtroom to sleep. At first I try to pay attention, but as Greig drones on, it becomes increasingly difficult to concentrate on what he's saying. Two of the jurors lean back in their chairs with eyes closed and the others look bored stiff.

No one appreciates a good argument more than I do. To me this is the most enjoyable part of a trial. Normally the only way I can get people to listen to me for more than fifteen minutes is to bind and gag them. But in a courtroom I have a captive audience. As much as the jurors would like, they can't run screaming from the courtroom, their hands covering their ears. But, as I also know, this captive audience has to be treated in a sensitive manner, not patronized or talked down to, not bored out of their skulls, but certainly not made to feel that we're on an equal footing. Naturally, I want them not only to like me but, just as important, to respect me. I feel that I'm like an instructor talking to a class- informative, convincing, entertaining, but also concise and clear. I try to speak with short easy sentences, explaining the evidence in a logical and reasonable manner so the jurors can fully understand it. But above all the jurors must feel that I believe what I am saying. I do my best to convey to the jury absolute sincerity.

I'm aroused from my thoughts by Greig raising his voice as he finalizes his argument. It appears as if he's now close to tears as he tells the jury, which is finally paying closer attention to him, about how embarrassed he was to find himself on the streets of Waikiki barred from the hotel where his wife was playing in a bridge tournament. About how he was in a state of tears after taking a cab home and calling his wife to tell her what happened. About how he was so shook up for the next several weeks that it was impossible for him to get any work done. He closes with a request that the jury award a mere $100,000 for the embarrassment, anxiety and emotional distress the hotel put him through, adding it's a sum the hotel can well afford to pay and certainly will never miss. The judge sustains my objection to Greig's argument about what the hotel can or cannot afford to pay, but I'm a little worried, noticing one or two of the jurors nodding their heads in agreement.

As soon as Greig is finished, the judge, without announcing the normal recess, nods to me to proceed. I stand up and start my closing argument.

"Your honor, ladies and gentlemen," I begin, "Although this case has proceeded quickly, please don't think that it's unimportant. It's certainly important to the plaintiff and to my client. But it's also important to the hotel industry in Honolulu and how they should or should not conduct themselves when situations such as this arise. What we ask is that you judge this case on the facts as testified to by the witnesses, by the instructions which will be given to you by the court, by the merits of the case and by your own common sense and everyday knowledge of human behavior. Please don't judge it by your emotions or by feeling sorry for one side or the other."

I notice three of the jurors nodding in agreement with me and continue, "I feel the crucial question for you to decide in this case is whether or not the hotel employees acted as reasonable people in the performance of their duties on the night in question. Did the bartender, seeing the plaintiff behaving in an offensive manner, act as a reasonable person by asking the plaintiff to leave? When the plaintiff persisted in acting loud and obnoxious, did the security officer act as a reasonable person by taking him to the security office, writing up a trespass form and calling a police officer to escort him off the premises? Did the hotel act reasonably in setting up its standards and guidelines in conjunction with other hotels in the city and the Honolulu Police department for removing customers who are drunk, disorderly or acting in an offensive manner? The court will instruct you that if the hotel and its employees did act reasonably then the verdict should be in their favor."

"I would suggest to you that not only did the hotel's employees act in a reasonable manner but that the plaintiff acted unreasonably and not as a reasonable person would have acted. The plaintiff testified that his wife was upstairs at a bridge tournament. Meanwhile, however, the evidence clearly indicates that he was in the bar getting drunk and trying to pick up two hotel guests. Certainly not the actions of a reasonable person. Then, when he's asked to leave them alone, he became obnoxious and belligerent. Again, not the actions of a reasonable person. Everything that happened to him that night was a result of his own behavior, was a natural reaction to his actions." At this point, Greig glares at me and his face turns an even darker red but, except for squirming in his chair, he makes no move to object.

Looking at the gallery, which has been filling up with spectators, I recognize several young associates from my law firm as well as several other attorneys. Law is one of the most theatrical of professions. All trial lawyers love to perform, and I'm no exception. So now I think I might as well pour it on a little.

I continue, "This is not a complicated case and normally I would stop here and let the judge instruct you so you can make your decision. But there is something I'd like to add, something that does bother me about this matter. Mr. Greig admitted to you that, when asked to leave, he told the hotel employees he was an attorney, would sue them and would end up owning the hotel. I certainly hope that you don't judge all attorneys by such remarks. In a way, I can have some empathy for Mr. Greig. No matter what you may think or may have heard, the practice of law is not easy. Most of the lawyers I know are hard working and put in long stressful hours on behalf of their clients. I'm certain that at one time Mr. Greig was among those honest, conscientious lawyers. But for some of us the stress and the hours take their toll and it certainly appears as if that's been the case with Greig."

Greig rises to his feet sputtering that he objects but he's unable to conjure up any grounds. The judge asks him to be seated and motions for me to continue. Again, Greig glares at me with eyes that are barely open and his face becomes as red as raw steak.

I continue. "But for the plaintiff to use the fact that he's a lawyer as a threat, and to add that he'd end up owning the hotel is inexcusable and on behalf of all hard working lawyers in this state I wish to apologize for that type of inappropriate behavior."

I conclude my argument and Park instructs the jury, directing them to retire to the jury room to start deliberations.

By the time I return to my office it's almost five. Park said he would keep the jury until it reaches a decision. We both feel it shouldn't take more than an hour or two. Maybe less. Marsha sets another cup of coffee in front of me. Only my tenth for the day. I tell myself that I have to cut back, that perhaps too much coffee is the reason I've been feeling so depressed lately. I hand her the Greig files to sort out and put away. She asks, "What do you think?"

"You never know what a jury will do, but I'd be surprised if they award him anything."

I look at my calendar and see that the trial set for Monday is Daniels vs. Lee. I try to recall the case but my mind is a complete blank. I don't remember anything about it. Maybe I have Alzheimer's. I ask Marsha to bring me the file and ask Frank to come in. She leaves and I place a call to Ken Ventura, claims manager for Hawaii Indemnity, the insurance carrier for the hotel.

"Ken. Mark. How are you?"

"Okay," he says, "How are you? How's the trial going?"

"I'm fine. We just argued and the jury is deliberating."

He laughs, "Damn. I thought closing arguments would be tomorrow. I wanted to be there."

"It went fast. You know how Park is. No fooling around. I'll come over for coffee in the morning."

"Sounds good to me. See you here about seven thirty?"

"Good. See you then."

We hang up. Ken is one of the best claims people I've ever dealt with. Honest, fair and decisive, but not inflexible. If the facts of a case change, he takes it in stride and acts accordingly. He's one of the few claims people I know who doesn't gag at the thought of paying a claim.

Frank walks in and almost falls down on the couch. He's as relaxed as a well-fed kitten while I watch my hand tremble as I pick up my coffee cup. I wonder what illness that signifies and wonder if I'm becoming a hypochondriac. I ask Frank how his case is going.

"Fine. Believe it or not I'm all ready to start tomorrow morning. Construction accident. A worker fell into a pit and broke his leg. Claims it wasn't well lit, no adequate railings and other OSHA violations. I think we have some good defenses. How's your trial going?"

Sardonically, I think to myself, here it is the day before trial and he actually knows what the case is about. But who am I to sneer? I don't have a clue as to what the Daniels case is about and it's just six days away. I ask, "No chance to settle?"

"None. The workers comp lien is larger than the case is worth. The Plaintiff's lawyer says he might as well try it."

"Okay. I've got a new case for you. Our client is Chicago Industries. The plaintiff is a sixteen year old football player on Maui. Apparently he was wearing a Chicago helmet, made a tackle and fractured his brain stem. He's now a quadriplegic."

Frank grimaces. "Shit! Poor kid!" Now that he's exhibited sympathy, which is only decent, he quickly shifts his focus to relevant legal concerns, and asks, "Any prior problems with their helmets?"

"Not according to their general counsel. I'll file an answer, get out some preliminary interrogatories and then turn it over to you for handling. But they want me to keep an eye on this one."

Frank smiles. "That's okay. It seems like you keep an eye on all of them."

Thinking to myself that he really doesn't give me much choice, I say, "Sorry, but I guess that's the way I am. Anyway it's your case."

"It's all right. I know I need looking after. Thanks. I like this kind of case. Makes me feel that my engineering degree wasn't a complete waste of time." Then he looks at his watch. Naturally it's a Rolex. "I've got to go. Final meeting with a witness before I leave."

"Good luck to you. If you need any help let me know."

As Frank leaves, Marsha enters carrying a pouch of files. She says, "The room always seems so much quieter when he's gone. Here's the file on the Lee case."

I smile but say nothing. She leaves the pouch on my desk and I gaze out the window at the now turquoise colored ocean and across the city at the sun-streaked slopes of Diamond Head. The ocean is dotted with sailboats, and though I'm no sailor I would love to be on one of them. Anywhere but here.

I turn back to the pouch and take out the correspondence file. All that's left are three huge volumes of medical records from Kaiser and one deposition. I look through the file and it still doesn't seem familiar. I think to myself that I'm getting as bad as Frank. Frightening thought! I try to concentrate on the papers in front of me. A rear-end auto accident. No wonder I couldn't remember it. We have dozens of them, mainly fender benders involving soft tissue type injuries to the neck or back. According to the file, this looks somewhat more serious, with substantial damage to both cars and a claimed disc problem with possible surgery in the future. I had earlier assigned it to Andrew Brown, a fairly new associate, to assist me in preparing for trial. I continue to look through the files and see that the last time I had periodically reviewed the file was two months ago. At the time I asked that he set up an Independent Medical Examination, but I see no report. There's no summary of the voluminous medical records, none of the doctors have been deposed and no subpoenas issued. I try to get Andy on the intercom but no answer. I again ask Marsha to come in.

"Can you find Andy for me?"

"Sorry, he's gone for the day. He always leaves by five."

"That's ridiculous," I almost shout. "Why hasn't anyone mentioned that to me?" I ask in a calmer voice not expecting an answer. "He was supposed to arrange for an independent medical exam on this case and never did."

"The one that's set for trial on Monday?"

"Yes. I'll look through the file now and give you the names and addresses of any witnesses we may need. Get the subpoenas out first thing tomorrow. Check with the clerk for a list of the plaintiff's subpoenas. Meanwhile, I'll look to see what else Andy may have forgotten to do."

Marsha sits down. "I hate to tell you this but I don't think he's going to make it. He comes in late, leaves early and every time I pass his office he seems to be day dreaming."

"Okay. Why don't you go home. I'll read this while waiting for the verdict."

I start to go through the file but have barely finished the correspondence when David Hunter and Julie Chung enter the room. David is in his early thirties, short and chubby with a round cheerful face. He's a former prosecutor from Newark who's found a home in Hawaii. Not too much experience in civil law but a good lawyer, intelligent, quick and witty. He's learning fast.

Julie was a psychiatric nurse who decided to go to law school after being knocked down too many times by out of control mental patients. She's been with us for almost two years. She's medium height, attractive, has a slender body which she keeps trim with early morning runs. I don't think she'll ever make it as a trial lawyer. She enters a courtroom as if it's a burning building but she's smart and hard working and is an excellent legal writer. Perfect for motions and disputes over insurance policies. She's also great at reviewing and summarizing medical records.

Both are hard workers and I feel fortunate they joined our firm. "How's the trial going?" David asks me.

"It's over except for the verdict. What's happening?"

Dave says, "I ran down that Rostky guy for you. I read the police report and I'll summarize it for you if you want."

"Police report? What happened?"

"Cohn didn't tell you? He was killed."

I look at him in disbelief. "When? How? What happened?"

Dave leans back, regarding me with the self-satisfied grin of someone who knows something important and intends to reveal it in an enticing way that suits him. "He was hit by a van."

"No kidding?" I reply, shocked and disbelieving.

Still grinning, he shakes his head and forces me to prod him, saying simply, "I kid you not."

"Come on. Tell me the whole story."

Dave smiles and starts in. "Okay. The van was in a high-speed chase. Apparently it had been stolen in Wahiawa and used in a burglary. Rostky was walking home from a bar along the shoulder of the road. There was no sidewalk. The van veered onto the shoulder and hit poor Rostky with such force that it not only shattered the windshield but actually decapitated him."

"My God! How awful." I look at my watch. It's almost six. I've been at it for almost twelve hours and thrown at me have been a quadriplegic, a broken leg, a possible back surgery, five minor injuries, a day in court with an aging alcoholic who was thrown out of a hotel and now a decapitation. Maybe it's not the coffee.

"There's more. His head fell onto the passenger seat of the van."

"You must be kidding. I bet Frank put you up to this."

"Absolutely not. It's the truth."

'You're telling me that the thief was trying to escape from the police and that Rostky's head was on the seat next to him. I don't believe you. Frank had to put you up to this." I look at Julie who's rolling her eyes in disbelief.

Dave repeats, "I'm telling the truth. It's even worse than that. The van was finally cornered in a dark field. The police surrounded the van with drawn guns. One of them opened the passenger door, stuck his pistol in Rostky's ear and ordered him to raise his hands."

With that all three of us burst into laughter.

Dave is gasping, "I swear to God. It's true. Ghastly, but true."

Julie looks at him and says, "No one, not even you, could make that up."

I agree. "No wonder Cohn wants to settle. He's got a dead client whose claim wasn't that good to start with."

"Not only that," says Julie, "but a recent case may give him a claim against the city. It imposes liability on the police for conducting high speed chases in populated areas."

"That's right," I agree, though the case made no particular impact on me at the time. I go on, "I'm meeting with Ventura in the morning. I'll try to get a few hundred for a quick settlement with Cohn."

Dave then asks, "Anything else happening?"

"Yes. I do have something I want to discuss with you but it must be kept confidential." They nod their heads and I continue, "It's about Andy. I have a case starting trial on Monday. I asked him to arrange for a medical exam of the plaintiff which he never did. He hasn't summarized the medical records and I see no reports to the carrier. I'm almost afraid to look at any other files I've assigned to him. I'd like you two to get a list of his files from Marsha and check them out for me. Please do it as soon as possible. I've also been told that his work hours are short, to say the least. I'm almost afraid to see what his billable hours look like. What do you think?"

They glance at each other, and I can tell they really don't want to answer the question, but Julie says, "I know he's having some problems with his wife. I don't think she likes it here and wants to return to Memphis. I guess that's where all her family and friends are."

"That's a common problem here," I reply. The husband is busy working, but the wife, if she isn't working, is away from her family and friends and gets lonely. They usually end up going home. How about you Dave? Does your wife want to return to Newark?"

He lets out a big laugh. "No way! She loves it here. She enjoys her job, has made lots of friends and is happier than she's been in years. The only problem is the cost of living. Everything is so damn expensive."

"You've got that right," Julie agrees. "Housing is out of sight. Food is so expensive, when I go to a grocery store on the mainland I feel everything is on sale."

I agree. "Yes, that's true. But on the other hand we don't have to spend as much for clothing, there are no heating bills and though gas is expensive we don't drive that far. My car is three years old and only has fourteen thousand miles on it." I then say, "I'm going to let Andy go tomorrow."

Julie answers. "I'm certain that his wife will be pleased. He's under a lot of pressure from her to return home. I know it's affecting his work."

"At any rate, please get that list from Marsha in the morning. I've got to look over this file."

Just then a voice on the intercom says, "The court clerk called. Your jury sent in a note that they've reached a verdict."

I stand up, grab my jacket and head for the door. "See you guys later."

"Wait," they both say, "We'll go with you."

The three of us dart out of the office and head for court.

Chapter 8

The morning following the Greig trial, I'm in my office drinking the worst coffee I've ever made. It's almost too thick to drink, more like gruel than coffee. Being the first one in does have its drawbacks.

Looking towards Diamond Head, I see the city light up as the sun rises over the ocean. Diamond Head is still a deep brown and will remain so until the winter rains begin. I sip my coffee thinking that I might as well inject pure caffeine into my veins as drink this junk. I dial Elaine's number. Busy. I hope she won't be too long. I'd like to talk to her while it's still quiet here.

Leaning back in my chair I think of her, of us. We first met when we were kids and the passion between us has not diminished over the years. Starting in elementary school, through high school and two years of college, through brutal arguments and fights, through marriages and children. When we're together, infrequent as it may be, it's as if we're kids again, as if no time has passed. There are no pretenses, no dishonesty, no games and no inhibitions.

And, I realize how utterly foolish it is. We're not kids and many years have passed. She has three children and has been married for almost twenty five years. Kathy and I have been contentedly married for eleven years. Yet, the thought of hearing her voice takes me back to those extraordinary days when all that mattered was being together. The thought of talking to her still excites me.

Looking at my watch I see that it's time for my meeting with Ventura. Reluctantly, I take the elevator to the lobby and walk across the street to his building. I go up to his floor, enter the door with the small 'claims department' sign, nod to the receptionist and walk back to Ventura's office. His secretary, Irene, fronts his room like a beefeater guard, but we're old friends and she tells me that I'm expected and she'll bring me a cup of coffee.

It's exactly 7:30 and I can see his out basket is already full. He's also an early riser. I greet him with a casual, "Good morning."

He totally dwarfs his chair. He's at least 6'3" and must weigh 240 pounds, all muscle. A former star defensive end on the University of Hawaii football team, in his mid-forties, he still works out everyday at the downtown YMCA on his lunch hour and looks as though he could take on most professional wrestlers. Good looking with large features, jet-black hair, he's smart and tough but still has compassion for the pain suffered by accident victims.

He looks up and smiles. "Hi. I see you're right on time as usual. Have a seat."

I also smile as I shift a large pile of folders from the only chair in his office to the floor. "I don't know if my phobia for never being late is a strength or a weakness, but I do have good news. The verdict came in last night. The jury found in favor of the hotel."

"Good," says Ken. "I was a little worried about that one. If he had come across as somewhat more sympathetic he might have won."

"I agree. But he's one of the least sympathetic people I've ever met. As a matter of fact", I laugh, "he's so unsympathetic that I almost felt sorry for him."

Ken's face lights up, "That bad?"

"Yes, actually I would've feel sorry for him but he acted like such an asshole at the hotel. By the way, remember the Rostky case?" Except for the final bill, The Greig case is already history.

"Vaguely. What about it?"

Irene strides into the room and hands me a styrofoam cup of hot coffee. I sip it as I repeat the story to him. As I tell him about the gun in the ear, Ventura explodes. "You're making it up!"

"No. It's the truth. The police report was on my desk this morning. I read it myself. What should we do with Cohn about the bar case? His last demand was $10,000 which we've always felt was too high."

Ventura looks at me quizzically, "Personally I don't think we should pay anything more than nuisance value to make it go away."

"I agree. Can I offer him a few hundred?"

"Make it up to $500.00. That should satisfy Cohn."

A Reasonable Person

As I nod my head in agreement, Irene walks in with two manila envelopes with letters attached by paper clips. Ventura scans the letters, signs them and hands me the envelopes. "Here's a couple of new files for you. Saves me the postage. How's your trial schedule?"

"Busy as hell. I have two or three scheduled every week well into next year. Frank is in trial right now. Not one of yours. Some kind of construction case. A worker fell into an open pit. He claims no warning sign or barricades."

Ken smiles and says, "Those are difficult to settle. Usually the worker comp lien is too high."

As usual he's absolutely right and I tell him so.

He adds, "Maybe you need some more associates to help you out."

He's been dealing with law firms for a long time. I say, "You're probably right, but it seems that as soon as I train one I need another. And finding lawyers who have the potential to be good trial lawyers is not that easy."

"That's true," he says. "There aren't that many good trial lawyers out there. I go regularly to claims managers meetings and they all say the same. That's why you and Frank are so busy."

"The problem is that anyone from the mainland who has trial experience wants too much money. Then I have to raise my hourly rates and you become unhappy. It seems to be a catch 22 situation. And the last thing I can do is turn down new cases. If I do, insurance carriers will stop sending me work."

Ventura shakes his head. "You're absolutely right. It's hard to convince the people upstairs that there are more important considerations in selecting law firms than hourly rates."

"What are these new cases about?" I ask. "Anything interesting?"

He smiles, "No. Just a couple of run of the mill auto accident cases."

"Then maybe I'll turn them over to David to handle. He seems to be working out alright and worked for several years as an assistant prosecuting attorney in Newark. He hasn't tried any civil cases but he does have trial experience."

"Sounds fine to me," Ken replies. Then we engage in some small talk as I finish my coffee. He asks me about my tennis game and I tell him I haven't been playing much. He tells me about a noon basketball league he joined at the 'Y' and suggests that I should give it consideration. We say goodbye and I return to my office thankful that I had some good news to give him.

Walter Davis

I go to the coffee room and pour myself a cup from a fresh pot. Sitting there are Frank, Julie and David. I say to Frank, "I thought you were in trial."

"It starts this afternoon. The judge had some motions to take care of."

As I sit, Marsha enters and hands me a large white envelope which looks like an invitation. I open it, read it and pass it on to Frank. It's an announcement that Robert J. Jeffries, Esq. has been appointed Honorary Counsel for the country of Upper Volta.

Reading it, he laughs and hands it to Julie. She laughs and hands it to David. "Who is Robert J. Jeffries and what is Upper Volta?" He asks.

I reply, "Bob was a classmate of mine at Law School. He's now practicing in L.A., but I've never heard of Upper Volta."

Frank smiles, "I've never heard of it either, but it sounds rather *electrifying* to me."

Julie chuckles, "Is their main export *batteries*?"

David adds, "No, it's probably *light bulbs*. Maybe the honorary counsel changes light bulbs."

I throw in, "I think you're all *shocking*." Everyone groans. "Come on, how many honorary counsels can Upper Volta have?"

Frank laughs, "Probably as many as it takes to screw in a light bulb."

Julie, smiling broadly, says, "I wonder if they have *circuit* courts. Watt do you think?"

I say, "I think you all belong in the *electric chair* or to be hit by *lightning*!"

We are now laughing and hardly notice that one of our file clerks has entered the room. Judi Ka'opuiki has worked for us since she graduated high school two years before. She's tall and thin with long black hair who would be attractive except for her large horn rimmed glasses and clothes which never quite fit. Initially, she worked as a receptionist and after a year was promoted to file clerk. She's taking para-legal courses at the local community college and, hopefully, will be our next para-legal. "What's so funny?" she asks.

Julie asks her, "Have you ever heard of Upper Volta?"

"Of course," she replies, "It's a small landlocked country in West Africa. Population almost 4 million, main economy is livestock and farming. It's a very poor country with a considerable amount of undeveloped mineral resources."

We stare at her with wide mouths. Julie asks, "How do you know that?"

She finishes pouring her coffee, and as she leaves the room mutters, "You people must think I'm not very smart."

Leaving the room I look at the others and say, "I thought we were the educated ones around here."

Frank adds, "Please don't forget to pay *ohmage* to your friend.'

The moment I enter my office the intercom announces an incoming call. Picking up the phone, I'm immediately asked to hold for Mr. Cohn. I hate it when secretaries tell me to hold and feel like hanging up but within seconds he's on the line. His voice is raspy from too many cigarettes. He doesn't even say hello. Instead it's, "Mark, it's Bill Cohn. Have you had a chance to look at the Rostky case?"

I slowly drawl, "Good morning, Bill. How are you today?"

"Fine, Mark." He rasps with rapid fire quickness. "What about Rostky?"

I laugh. "You mean your dead client? Are you going to dismiss? By the way, you may have a good case against the county. There's a new supreme court case involving rules for high speed chases."

He replies, "I saw it, but can't we settle the bar case?" I'm now positive that he wants to resolve the bar case so he can proceed against the county.

I ask him, "How much do you want."

He says, "My original demand was $10.000.00 but now I'd take $1,000.00."

Being in a hurry to settle, I tell him the most we'll go is $500.00 and he agrees, sounding pleased, which means I should have offered less. As I'm dictating a memo to Marsha instructing her to get a check and the proper releases from Ventura, the intercom announces another call.

I settle another case and look at the two new cases which Marsha has put on my desk. I call in Dave and hand him the files, telling him, "Here are two new cases for you to handle. I know you're busy but we're looking for a new associate. Do you know of anyone who might be interested?"

He says, "No. But I'll keep my eyes open."

The intercom interrupts us announcing a collect call from San Rafael, California. Elaine! I ask Dave to leave, pick up the phone and tell the operator that I'll accept the charges.

"Hello," we say together.

There's a moment of silence, then, "How are you?" She asks.

"I've been good. Your voice sounds great. How are you?"

"I'm fine. I called because I want to thank you for such a wonderful afternoon. I wish we could get together more often."

It was a good afternoon. "It was great for me too," I say, trying to bury the nagging feeling of guilt that burdens me.

"When will I see you again?" She asks. "Will you be returning to San Francisco soon?"

"I doubt it," I reply. "I have trials scheduled every week. I don't know when I'll be able to get away."

She sighs, "I miss you already. Please see what you can do. Promise me you'll try."

"I'll try, but it won't be soon. I'm really tied up."

"Please try," She repeats and then, "I'm sorry but I've got to go. I have to take my daughter to the doctor."

"Is she alright?" I ask.

"Just a sore throat, but I'm running late. I'll call you next week. Hopefully, I'll have more time. What's a good day?"

"I start a trial on Monday. Friday at this time would be good."

"I'll call you then," she says. "Bye. I love you." Her voice trails off. It's clear that she wants something but doesn't want to discuss it on the phone.

"Me too. Goodbye." I hang up, lean back in my chair and wonder what the hell is going on with her.

Chapter 9

The Greig case is now behind me, and a new day in court has begun. It's precisely 8:30 on Monday morning as the bailiff orders all to stand and announces that the Circuit Court for the First Circuit of the State of Hawaii is now in session, the Honorable Lester Sakumoto, judge presiding. The judge sits as do the lawyers and prospective jurors.

Judge Sakumoto belongs to that select group of Hawaiian born Japanese-Americans who fought with the 442nd in Europe. He was given a field commission and a silver star for bravery. After the war he completed college and law school, went to work in the state attorney's office giving legal advice and opinions to various state bureaucrats. Thanks more to his friendship with the governor and prominent members of the legislature, than to his legal ability or experience, he was appointed to the circuit court.

Judge Sakumoto is one of the largest men of Japanese descent I've ever seen. Over six feet and weighing at least 240 he is, to say the least, imposing. But his voice and his mannerisms are gentle for a man of his size, and he's polite and courteous to everyone in his courtroom. I've never seen him lose his temper. As far as I'm concerned, this more than makes up for his lack of trial experience.

Sitting next to me is my client, a very nervous Mrs. Lee, wife of one of the most renowned cardio-vascular surgeons in the state. She's a small woman in her early forties, petite and delicate. Pursuant to instructions from our office she's conservatively dressed in a black skirt and grey blazer. Her only jewelry, in addition to her wedding ring, is a watch and a simple shell necklace. She's an attractive Asian who, while momentarily distracted, ran into the rear of a car driven by Mr. Daniels. We met this morning for the first time outside the courtroom. I try to give the proposed jurors the impression that I've been her family lawyer for years.

In front of me, on the counsel table, are my files including three thick volumes of medical records subpoenaed from Kaiser Medical Center. The plaintiff's lawyer did not order copies. Big mistake.

My entire weekend was spent reviewing these files from cover to cover as well as reading and re-reading all medical reports. I look across at the plaintiff, Robert Daniels, and his attorney. Daniels, according to his deposition, is fifty-two, a burly pipe fitter at Pearl Harbor, divorced with no children. The tight fitting corduroy suit he's wearing is not well tailored. He looks like he's having trouble breathing in it.

Sitting next to him is his attorney, Jason Ing, about thirty, of Chinese-American descent, sharply dressed in a charcoal gray suit and maroon tie. His boss, George Ching, isn't here, which leaves me somewhat puzzled. Ching is an old timer, an excellent trial lawyer, and I wonder why he allows this case to be tried by an inexperienced associate. Probably because he was told it's a slam-dunk and Ing can use the experience.

After the preliminary opening remarks by Sakumoto, we get down to the business of selecting a jury. Ing asks a few perfunctory questions and it's my turn. Normally, I consider jury selection second in importance only to closing argument since it's the only time during a trial where a dialogue can take place between lawyer and juror. Also, it can be a good chance to argue your side of the case under the guise of asking questions concerning their bias to sit as jurors. However, in this case, I don't want to spend a lot of time in jury selection so I limit my questioning. I ask if they have any quarrel with the concept that the plaintiff must prove his case by a preponderance of the evidence, about whether any of them have been injured in accidents and talk to them about using their common sense in reaching a decision.

One of the jurors raises his hand. I look at my jury sheet and see that his name is Donald Stanford, he's forty-three, a divorced construction worker. It appears that he has much in common with Daniels. There's no way I want him on the jury. "Mr. Stanford," I ask him, "Do you have a comment you'd like to make?"

"Yes sir," he replies. "I was in an accident several years ago and injured my back. It still hurts."

A Reasonable Person

I ask, "Do you think that might affect your ability to reach a fair and impartial verdict in this case?" Then I add, gratuitously, "You understand that all both sides are asking for is a fair shake?"

Stanford shakes his head. "I don't know. As I said, my back still hurts." It's clear that what he really wants is to get out of here. I know exactly how he feels.

At this point, Sakumoto dismisses him and calls the next name on the list.

The entire process takes less than two hours. It looks like a good jury consisting of seven women, the usual mix of school teachers, utility and government workers and retirees. Unfortunately, businessmen and professionals are invariably excused.

Judge Sakumoto calls for a fifteen-minute recess and asks counsel to meet with him in chambers. I give Mrs. Lee a farewell hug under the watchful eyes of the jury and follow Ing into chambers. Sakumoto is already out of his robe and in the bathroom. We sit and I ask Ing how his boss is feeling and why he isn't here.

Ing replies, "George feels this is a fairly easy case for me to gain some experience."

I ask, "How many jury cases have you tried?"

"Actually, this is my first. But I did second chair George on several."

His manner and tone of voice are casual and relaxed, but his eyes reveal intense hostility born of fear, the fear of failure. As he says this, he looks as though he wants to grind me into chopped liver. Fortunately, I have a very thick skin. I smile hoping to get under his skin. "Try not to be too hard on me."

He looks away as the judge enters the room and sits at his desk which looks much smaller now that his overwhelming figure is behind it. The judge eyes us, somewhat balefully. "Well, gentlemen, any chance of this case settling. It certainly doesn't appear to be too complicated."

Ing hurriedly pipes up. "It's a simple rear-ender, judge. My client has a disc problem which will undoubtedly require surgery. The case is worth no less than $100,000. He looks at me as if expecting that I will simply write out a check. When I don't he almost looks disappointed.

The judge asks me, "How much authority do you have?"

I have a letter in my file authorizing me to offer $30,000 but I look at the judge and say, "25,000."

Sakumoto asks me, "Can you get $50,000?"

"Sorry, judge, but I tried for that this morning and was turned down."

That's already two lies and the trial hasn't even started.

Again, Ing jumps in. "My client wouldn't accept $50,000 even if offered." He goes on to repeat himself. "His injury is worth no less than $100,000."

The judge looks at me and I simply shake my head. He shrugs and says. "Alright, let's get started. How long is it going to take?"

"Thursday, I'd say, your honor." Ing agrees. The judge looks around the room and my eyes follow. He has a complete set of golf clubs in the corner with his putter leaning against the wall. Typically Japanese, he loves his golf and is obviously more concerned about his golf game than he is about this trial.

The rest of the morning is taken up with the testimony of the investigating police officers. They testify that from the positions and damages of the respective vehicles and from the statements of the parties that Daniels' vehicle, while stopped for traffic on Kapiolani Blvd., was struck from the rear by Mrs. Lee's vehicle. If Ing had asked I would have stipulated to that. My cross examination of the officers is short, but I do get them to testify that this was a routine fender-bender, that neither party complained of injuries and there was no need to call for an ambulance.

During the lunch break, I remain in the courtroom. I can think of no place that is more peaceful. Once again I review the medical records of Daniels' treating physician. Dr. Stone is a family doctor with offices near Pearl Harbor who reports that, as a result of the accident, Daniels is suffering from low back pain which will require surgery. His bill amounts to almost $4,000.00, most of which is for physical therapy.

I also look through the Kaiser records, though I'd spent almost the entire weekend reviewing them. Kathy is hardly speaking to me. All of our weekend plans were cancelled for this case. She's usually fairly patient, but this time she definitely was not happy. It's so damn hard to explain. So many cases. I simply don't have time during the week to read this stuff. I know it's hard on her, but I can't go into court unprepared. And this case is especially difficult since Andy had done almost nothing by way of preparation. No independent medical examination. No deposition of the treating physician. No review or outline of the voluminous records from Kaiser. I look at the Kaiser records and thank God for small favors.

After lunch, Ing tells me that he has a representative from an auto body shop to testify as to the repair estimate for Daniels' car. I tell him that I'll stipulate to the amount and for a moment he looks as though he actually likes me. That feeling won't last much longer.

The next witness is Dr. Richard Stone. Dr. Stone is a slender individual in his mid fifties. He's not board certified, but has practiced medicine for over twenty-five years. He takes most of the afternoon testifying as to the injuries sustained by Daniels and the treatment he's received. He also testifies that in his opinion all of Daniel's injuries were caused by this accident, that the prognosis is not good and Daniels will most probably require back surgery.

By the time he's through, Judge Sakumoto looks tired and announces that court is adjourned and for everyone to return at 8:30 A.M. the following morning. The courtroom is now empty except for Ing and myself.

He approaches me and smiles. "Are you sure you don't want to settle? I think the jury may award more than one hundred thousand. Hawaiian jurors have been very liberal lately" He's more relaxed now, seems confident that he'll win, and doesn't regard me with such hostility.

He's right about Hawaiian jurors. They've been paying off like slot machines in the past few years resulting in some of the highest verdicts in the country. But I smile back. "I don't think so. I think it will be more in the range of our offer. But it doesn't matter. The carrier refuses to give me any more authority." I don't tell him I haven't asked.

"Then I guess I'll see you in the morning. Can I tell Dr. Strong how long your cross examination will take?"

"Tell him no more than an hour. See you in the morning."

I watch him leave. He seems like a nice guy, and I almost feel sorry for him. But in this business you must do your homework. I head back to the office, knowing that I have at least two hours of paperwork to do and that our associates are waiting to talk. With Kathy feeling as she does, I'd rather not go home, but then I'd be in real trouble.

Back in my office, with a fresh cup of coffee in front of me, I call home and Kathy answers. Andy Brown enters the room and I motion for him to sit. Kathy, sounding friendlier than she had this morning, asks me when I'll be home.

She says, "I just got home. How about meeting at the Outrigger for dinner."

Hugely relieved that she's no longer boiling with resentment, I tell her that dinner out sounds great and I apologize again for neglecting her over the weekend. She replies, "I'm sorry I got angry but you work too hard. When will you be through?"

"I'll be there by seven." We say goodbye and I turn to face Andy. I ask him, "How are things going?"

He says, "I think I have to quit. My wife is not happy here. She wants to return home and is driving me crazy. I know my work is suffering."

I feel as if I've been let off the hook. Now I don't have to fire him. "To be honest, Andy, you didn't do a very good job on the Lee case. You did absolutely no preparation at all and caused me to spend the entire weekend going over it."

He looks as if he's going to burst into tears, "I'm truly sorry, but this thing with my wife has really been getting to me."

I ask him, "When will you be leaving?"'

He replies, "Would two weeks be alright?"

The last thing I want is for him to hang around for two weeks doing nothing. "Andy, I think it would be best if you leave tomorrow. I'll have Ellen get you a check for two weeks pay. I've had Dave and Julie look over the cases you were assigned and they can handle them until we replace you."

He looks like he wants to talk some more but I just don't have the time. I stand up and extend my arm to shake hands with him. "Good luck Andy. I hope you do better on your next job."

He shakes my hand and says, "I'm sure I will. Again, I'm sorry for letting you down." He leaves my office obviously downcast. I only hope he doesn't ask me for a reference.

As he leaves Dave enters the room. The two associates nod at each other. When Andy is out of earshot, David sits down and says, "He didn't look too good."

"He quit. He'll be gone tomorrow. Can you and Julie handle his caseload until we hire a replacement?"

He looks at me and smiles, "No problem. We're already on it. How's the trial going?"

"As planned. We selected the jury and gave opening statements. The police officers and treating doctor testified. Tomorrow I'll cross-examine his doctor and the plaintiff will testify. Thanks to Andy, I have no witnesses. We can settle instructions and argue on Wednesday. Judge Sakumoto will be pleased. He won't have to miss his Thursday afternoon golf game."

A Reasonable Person

Dave grins, "I hear he really likes his golf. Do you know that Judge Azeka has set a pre-trial conference in the Andrews vs. Beach Hotel case on Friday morning? Trial starts Monday. When can we talk?"

I look at my calendar and sure enough there it is. I vaguely recall the case. I took the depositions of the plaintiff and her psychiatrist about a year before in Los Angeles. Ms. Andrews seemed like a nice person, sincere and truthful. My thinking at the time was that the case should settle.

"Why not have Julie bring in the file and we can talk now. I don't have to leave for another hour." I get Julie on the intercom and ask her to come in. Two minutes later she enters with a folder and sits down. As they tell me about the case, I scan through my correspondence which is now piled high on my desk.

Dave begins. "You probably recall that the plaintiff is a forty-three year old single woman from Los Angeles who was staying by herself at the Beach Hotel. Her room was on the ninth floor. All of the rooms have lanais. She claims she was raped by a young man who entered her room through the lanai door. Here are some photos of the back of the hotel."

By now I'm giving them my full attention. David hands me six pictures showing the back of the hotel with the plaintiff's room marked in red. I look at them and say, "It looks impossible! How could anyone climb up there? I don't think a monkey could do it."

Julie says, "That's what we think. Dave and I went to the hotel to see for ourselves and it's hard to believe that anyone could have climbed up to her lanai. You took her deposition and reported that she seemed sincere and truthful, but I find her difficult to believe."

"I also took the deposition of her psychiatrist. How do you feel about his testimony?"

Julie takes the deposition out of the folder. "It's hard to say. He claims post-traumatic stress syndrome with the usual symptoms. He testified that with proper treatment she should be all right. I'm sure you remember, she's a school teacher in Santa Monica and took off work for about six months."

I couldn't even remember what she looked like but nodded my head at Dave and Julie as if I were way ahead of them. I'm sure they know better. "Go on. Tell me more."

"The judge ordered her to return to Honolulu before trial for an evaluation by a psychiatrist of our choice. We've made arrangements for Dr. Bertram to see her on Thursday. All of the updated records were sent to Bertram last week. If we want, we can re-depose her on Friday."

I ask, "Who are their witnesses?"

Dave answers, "The plaintiff, her psychiatrist, the emergency room doctor who saw her right after the incident, the head of security for the hotel and the director of security for the hotel chain. They took the deposition of the head of security but not of the director. Also, they've subpoenaed all police reports having to do with any crime that took place at the hotel for the past three years. I've completely reviewed them and there have been no previous rapes."

"What type of crimes were there?" I ask. "How many?"

"A few burglaries but none by entry through a lanai. Some assault and batteries, but these took place in public areas. Some slip and falls which our office is handling. Nothing really serious."

Julie adds, "Our only witnesses are the manager of the hotel and Dr. Bertram."

"I've never met Bertram. What's he like?"

She replies, "He should be a good witness. He's a Harvard grad who took his residency at Mass General. Very impressive credentials. The plaintiff's attorney is taking his deposition on Friday. Do you want to attend?"

I look at my calendar. "No. Why don't you do it. I have a deposition on Friday afternoon. As a matter of fact, you should probably second-chair me. You can handle the psychiatric testimony."

Julie blanches, "I don't think I'm ready for that."

Both Dave and I break out laughing. When she sees I'm kidding she gets her color back and smiles, "Very funny. But I will prepare some questions for you."

I get up to leave. It's almost time to meet Kathy.

Entering the main dining room of the Outrigger Canoe Club, I look around for Kathy and find her sitting at our favorite table by the wall, overlooking the water. I place a fresh ginger lei around her neck and kiss her cheek. She looks lovely and I tell her so. Her brightly colored Hawaiian V-neck dress is embellished with stone and bead detailing to add a little sparkle. Smiling, she asks where I picked up the lei.

"At a little shop in Chinatown. That's why I'm late."

She knows better but fingers it and says, "Thank you. It's very pretty. I'm glad I suggested this. We don't go out for dinner alone much anymore. In fact, we don't seem to do much of anything together anymore."

I look at her and realize she's right. "I know. It's just that I've been so damn busy. My trial schedule is almost out of control. The insurance companies are getting tighter and tighter yet verdicts are high, so plaintiff's lawyers want to go to trial. I feel like I'm caught in the middle."

She looks at me with sympathy but also what appears to be speculation, as though she's trying to read me. "I feel fortunate just to have a quiet dinner alone with you. Are you sure there's no more to it than that? Just too much work?" She's fishing.

I smile and shake my head, feigning surprise, "Do you think I'm having an affair?"

She pauses before replying, looks down at the ring on her finger, then raises her eyes and says, "No, Not yet."

The older I get, the more I believe in female intuition. Somehow a women always knows when there's another woman in the picture, even if it's she's just in a man's mind. "What does that mean? That I'm thinking of having an affair?"

"Maybe. You certainly haven't been having much of an affair with me recently."

I try to cover my anxiety about being suspected and possibly found out with a broad lascivious grin. "You've got that right, I'm sorry to say. But we can make up for lost time, can't we? What do you think the lei and wine are all about? I have some very lewd plans for us after dinner."

"She leers back at me and responds, "Not nearly as lewd as my plans are. And who said I need a lei or wine? Or dinner?"

I stand up and take her hand. "Let's get the hell out of here. Remember the times we'd have great sex followed by scrambled eggs? I hope you're in the mood for scrambled eggs."

She rises and as we walk quickly out of the dining room, she says, "I'm always in the mood for scrambled eggs after great sex."

She was on the scent, but I'd managed to divert her. At least there was no confrontation, not for the time being anyway. Sometimes it's difficult for me to analyze my own feelings. At this moment, I feel powerfully drawn to Kathy, and I really am looking forward to getting into bed with her. She's a wonderful lover, uninhibited and always responsive. And she deserves a man who can focus entirely on her, not someone whose thoughts may stray to another woman. So I tell myself as I try in vain to exclude Elaine from my thoughts.

Chapter 10

Kathy and Elaine are both excluded from my thoughts as I enter the courtroom the following morning. I'm fifteen minutes early, and the only person in the room is Mrs. Lee, sitting at the counsel table. Her eyes are dark-ringed and she looks haggard. I sit next to her, spread out my files and greet her. "Good morning. How are you today?" The jury isn't in yet so no hug.

It looks like she's been up all night but she manages to smile. "Good morning. I've been up most of the night worrying."

I try to give her an optimistic smile. "No need to worry. First of all, if we lose, your insurance carrier will pay the judgment. Second, we're not going to lose."

"You sound like my husband. He told me last night that his medical malpractice insurance costs him a small fortune and he's never had a claim. He's not too concerned about this but I am."

The jurors are entering the courtroom so I pat her shoulder and again tell her not to be concerned.

At 8:30 AM Judge Sakumoto takes his place and the trial resumes. Dr. Stone is on the stand. My cross-examination is brief and to the point. Stone testifies that he never saw or treated Daniels before the auto accident, that he never reviewed any of Daniels' prior medical records including those of Kaiser Medical Center, that his medical opinion concerning Daniels' injuries was based solely on his physical examination and the history given to him by Daniels. Daniels told him that he never had any prior back problems, had no previous treatment for his back and had never been in an accident before Mrs. Lee struck his car from the rear.

looking at the jury, I slowly ask one last question. "Doctor, if the plaintiff had told you that he'd been in a number of accidents and had been treated numerous times for prior back injuries would your opinion still be the same, that is, that his back problems and necessity for surgery were the result of his accident with Mrs. Lee?" I wait for an objection but there is none. Unbelievable!

Apparently, Dr. Stone has more trial experience than Jason Ing. He's also waiting for an objection and finally realizing that Ing isn't going to object says, "If that were true I'd certainly have to re-evaluate my opinion, but Mr. Daniels told me that there were no previous accidents and I have no evidence that there were any." As he says this, he looks at Ing and shakes his head in an expression of disbelief.

At this point Ing finally jumps up and shouts, "Objection! Assuming facts not in evidence."

Sakumoto looks at him with disgust, "Too late, Mr. Ing. The question has already been asked and answered. Please call your next witness."

Shamed and contrite, Ing calls his client to the stand.

Daniels is a big man, well over six feet tall, and it appears as if he weighs about 250 pounds. Mainly blubber. He comes across as belligerent, over-bearing and obnoxious. Not a very good witness under the best of circumstances, and this is not going to be the best of circumstances for him.

Having been shamed by the judge, Ing stumbles his way through direct examination. Daniels testifies about his back pain, the fact that he couldn't work for a long period of time after the accident, how the back pain has completely ruined his life style including his social life and his sex life and how, though he's afraid of surgery, that his back hurts so much that he's willing to undergo an operation. He further testifies that he never had problems with his back before Mrs. Lee's car struck him from the rear and had never been in a prior accident.

By the time he's through, Sakumoto recesses for lunch and orders everyone to return at 1:30PM. Returning to my office, I'm reading my mail and finishing a sandwich as Frank walks in. I ask him how his trial is going.

He flops down on my couch and says, "Not bad. We settle instructions and argue this afternoon. I think the plaintiff will be found more than 50% negligent. He disobeyed every safety rule in the book."

I nod. Hawaii is a comparative negligence state. If the jury finds the plaintiff more than 50% negligent it's a defense verdict. "Let's hope so. I may get a defense verdict, too."

"How can you do that? Isn't it a clear rear-ender?"

"I think I'll show that his injuries weren't caused by the accident."

Frank looks at me in disbelief. "I've heard how Andy screwed up with this one. You have no medical evidence, do you?"

I get up to return to court and as I'm walking out the door, I mutter, "I'm going to show that the plaintiff is a fucking liar."

It's exactly 1:30 as Sakumoto resumes his seat and his law clerk calls the court to order. The judge looks at me and says, "Mr. Dorsey, Do you wish to cross-examine?"

"Yes, your Honor, I do." Boy, do I!

I take Volume One of the Kaiser records to the podium as Daniels retakes the witness stand. In my first line of questioning he repeats that he had no prior accidents and had never been treated for back problems before his accident with Mrs. Lee. He further admits that he didn't complain of injuries at the scene and didn't see Dr. Stone until two weeks after the accident. I then ask, "Have you been treated at Kaiser Medical Clinic for any physical problems?"

He replies, "Yes. Mainly for colds."

I hold up volume one of the Kaiser records and walk to counsel table. Showing an obvious effort, I lift the equally weighty volumes two and three of the records. "Do you get many colds?"

Daniels replies, "Well, I've had the flu a number of times."

Looking at the jury, I smile. They smile back. I then turn to a pre-marked page and ask, "Do you recall going to the emergency room at Kaiser on May 5, 1966, with complaints of lower back pains saying that you had been in an auto accident that day?"

Ing stands up and demands to see the records. I hand him a copy of the emergency room records and turn back to Daniels as I read from the records. "Is your name Robert Daniels and on May 5, 1966, was your address 1026 Peacock Lane?"

"Yes. But I don't recall going to emergency."

Handing additional copies of the medical records to Ing and to the clerk, I ask that they be marked for identification. I then ask, "Mr. Daniels, according to these records you were treated for low back problems for two months at which time your doctor wrote a report to an insurance carrier that your back problems were permanent. Do you recall that?"

"No."

"Are you denying that these records pertain to you?"

"No. But I must have completely recovered."

"I'm sure we're all pleased for you," I say sarcastically. Turning back to the records, I hand Ing and the clerk copies of more pages. I then ask Daniels, "Do you recall being involved in an accident at work on June 8, 1968?"

"No."

"Let me refresh your memory. According to these records you went to Kaiser on June 9, 1968, claiming that on the previous day you strained your low back due to lifting some heavy pipes. Do you recall that?"

"No."

"Apparently you were off work for almost four weeks, were treated for four months and filed for worker compensation benefits claiming permanent injuries to your back. Do you remember that?"

He's not quite so arrogant as he says, "Vaguely. But I recovered, so it's not too clear to me at this time."

I look at the jury. They're all smiling now. But it's far from over. Turning to my next marker, I resume my questioning. "According to these records, you also went to the emergency room at Kaiser on August 18, 1970, claiming that you tripped on the steps at the Waikiki Theatre. You complained of low back pain, were treated for six months and filed an insurance claim stating that you sustained a permanent low back problem. Do you remember that?"

Daniels has by now sunk very low in the witness chair. "I think so."

More pages are marked for identification and shown to Daniels. "Are you the Robert Daniels referred to in the records?" He admits that he is.

Picking up volume 2 of the medical records, I turn to a pre-marked page. Two of the men on the jury actually start laughing. I look at Ing who's sagging in his chair looking like someone has mortally wounded him. Although I feel sorry for him he needed to be taught a lesson. Next time he'll read all of the records. Before I can ask another question the judge calls a fifteen minute recess and asks counsel to join him in chambers.

When we enter, the judge is sitting behind his desk with a menacing frown. He says to Ing, "What's the matter with you? Why weren't you familiar with the Kaiser records?"

Ing looks like he's going to break into tears. "I've never seen them. I didn't know they were subpoenaed."

I show Sakumoto the certificate from the court reporter's office proving that Ing had been notified of the subpoena. He looks at it and says scornfully to Ing, "Obviously you were notified. You just didn't order a copy. You probably thought they were insignificant. That's an unforgivable error." He then turns to me, "Is the $25,000 still on the table?"

"No judge. The carrier withdrew all authority when our offer was turned down yesterday." I can almost see my nose starting to grow but there's no way I want to settle now.

Sakumoto frowns. "Call the carrier. See how much you can get."

Even though it's well known that Sakumoto is very pro-plaintiff, it's still surprising that he'd want a liar like Daniels to walk away with any money at all. Nonetheless, I tell him that I'll call. He tells me to use the phone in the outer office.

Placing the call, I'm told that the claims manager is at a meeting on Maui and can't be reached. When I return to Sakumotos' office, the judge is practicing his putting on the carpet trying to hit a golf ball into a coffee cup about fifteen feet away. Ing turns toward me with a hopeful expression on his face.

I say, "Sorry, judge. The claims manager is unavailable and he's the only one who can extend authority."

Clink! The ball hits the cup. Sakumoto asks, "When can you talk to him?" He hits another ball at the cup.

"Tomorrow morning."

Clink! This one also strikes its mark. "Then we'll recess until 9:00AM tomorrow and I hope you have some good news." We go out to the courtroom and the judge dismisses the jury until 9:00AM the following day. I explain to Mrs. Lee and return to my office to start preparing for the rape case.

It's almost six and my desk is fairly clear. My dictation over the past two hours fills three tapes. That should keep Marsha busy tomorrow. I call Kathy and tell her I'll be home in an hour. She says she's baking a chicken, which reminds me that except for a sandwich at noon I've had nothing to eat all day. I can almost smell the chicken through the phone. I glance through my phone messages but see nothing that I can't return until my trial is over.

David and Julie enter and I motion for them to sit and ask, "How's the rape case coming along?"

David answers. "It looks good. We've completed the jury instructions and the security guys will be here tomorrow evening at six."

Julie adds, "The deposition of Dr. Bertram is scheduled for Friday afternoon. I'm meeting with him beforehand."

"Sounds good to me. What's happening with Frank's trial?"

Julie answers. "He's at court now. The jury had a question."

David quips. "They probably want to know the name of his barber. How's your trial coming along?"

We all smile. Leaning back I look out my window. The city is beginning to turn dark, and I see the sparkle of the dinner cruise boats as they make their nightly way to the waters off Waikiki. I say, "Not too bad. The judge called us into chambers and practically ordered me to settle. I have to call Granger in the morning."

"Are you going to settle?"

"I'm going to try to talk Granger out of it." Richard Granger is the claims manager for Mrs. Lee's insurance company. "He usually agrees with my recommendations."

David asks, "Why don't you want to settle?"

"Because the guy testified that he had no prior problems and I found six in the Kaiser records. I've asked him about three so far and the jury is starting to laugh at him. It should be a defense verdict."

Just then Frank sticks his head in the door. "Speaking of defense verdicts, I just got one! The jury found the plaintiff 65% negligent. I've got to call Lynn. We're going out to celebrate."

We all congratulate him as he leaves. I turn back to my associates. "I'm so tired I can hardly keep my eyes open. "What do we have after the rape case?"

This time it's David. "The Ferraro case. Mrs. Ferraro is an Avon lady in Kailua. She stuck her head over the gate of our clients' house to see if anyone was answering the doorbell and got half of her face ripped off by the family Akita."

I actually remember this one. The photos of the plaintiffs' face were gruesome. I'm too tired to discuss it now. Getting up to leave, I tell them, "Let's talk about it tomorrow. I'm out of here."

CHAPTER 11

It's eight, the following morning, and I'm on the phone trying to settle a case with Steve Goldberg. Steve, a Harvard grad, is one of the most competent personal injury lawyers in Honolulu. He's intelligent, thorough and tough in court but very pleasant and always a gentleman.

Steve represents a young boy who was seriously burned in a Waikiki restaurant while celebrating his twelfth birthday. His mother ordered a flaming dessert and the waiter, while lighting the brandy, set the boys' shirt on fire. The boy suffered serious burns over the upper part of his torso. He's had a number of surgeries and the scarring is dreadful.

Apparently the waiter's lighter ignited the vapors turning the brandy bottle into an instant flame thrower. Fortunately, the waiter had the good sense to immediately grab a table cloth from a nearby table and wrap it around the boy to extinguish the fire. Without a doubt this saved him from even more serious injuries. However, the waiter was responsible for the accident by not following correct procedures. The insurance carrier for the restaurant has given me authority to settle for up to $250,000 plus all necessary medical bills. Steve's last demand was $350,000.

"Steve," I say with all the sincerity I can muster up at this time of the morning, "I just got off the phone with the insurance carrier and they've given me $100,000 to settle."

At this point, many lawyers might get upset with me, but Steve remains calm. Although he knows I'm not quite telling the truth he also knows that this is the way the game is played. Since he hasn't taken the depositions of the waiters he doesn't know the entire story. I can visualize his broad smile as he says, "Mark, you know my clients will never agree to $100,000. Your people have to come up with more than that."

Looking at my watch, I say "Remember they're also going to pay all medical bills and he can go anywhere he wants for treatment. Steve, I've got to be in court soon. Give me a lower figure I can take back and I promise I'll present it to them." We both know that lawyers can be severely reprimanded, maybe even disbarred, for not presenting all offers to their clients so I'm not conceding much.

Steve laughs. "I'll tell you what. I'll recommend $300,000 but not a dime less. When can you get back to me?"

Now I'm certain he'll accept the $250,000 and maybe even less. I tell him I'll call him tomorrow, say goodbye, hang up and call Granger.

I tell Granger about the Lee trial and he sounds incredulous. "You mean to say he's had six prior accidents and lied about all of them. I've never heard of such a thing. What do you want to do?"

"I want you to withdraw all authority and order me to finish the trial whether I like it or not."

He says, "I hereby withdraw all authority and I'm ordering you to finish the trial whether you like it or not. But you'd better get a defense verdict."

We both laugh and I tell him, "I'll call you for lunch when the trial is over." We say goodbye and I head for court.

Knocking on the judge's door, I hear a loud "enter!" Sakumoto is still practicing his putting. He must be the best putter in Hawaii. "Well," he says, "Is the case settled?"

"No, your honor," I respond. "The insurance company has instructed me to proceed with the trial."

I can see that he doesn't know whether to believe this or not. He asks, "Who are you dealing with?"

"Richard Granger at First Hawaiian."

Now he believes me. Granger has a well deserved reputation of being one tough guy to deal with. "OK. Let's get on with it."

In the courtroom I greet my client who is still drained but less anxious looking. Hearing Daniels exposed by my cross-examination has given her hope, and I try to radiate confidence as I give her a good morning hug.

Ing looks at me and I shake my head. He looks dejected, as the judge enters the courtroom. Daniels resumes the witness stand. The judge reminds him that he's still sworn to tell the truth. I smile. The jury laughs. I go through the next three accidents with Daniels who by now is willing to say anything to get off the stand. One look at the grinning jurors and I know it's a defense verdict. He should be charged with perjury but Sakumoto would never do that. I finish my cross-examination and Daniels retreats from the witness stand not daring to look at the jury. Lee rests and so do I. There's no need to have Mrs. Lee testify.

The jury is dismissed until 1:30PM, and Ing and I enter the judge's office to settle jury instructions. Most are standard so it only takes about thirty minutes. We're also told to return at 1:30PM for closing arguments and I return to my office where a turkey sandwich is waiting for me on my desk along with what seems like a ton of new paperwork.

Leaning back in my chair, I take a huge bite of my sandwich as Frank enters. He takes a seat on my couch and asks about my trial. I tell him what happened and he shakes his head in disbelief. "I agree. It should be a defense verdict." He stands up to go. "I have to run. I'm taking Ben Chang for lunch. He wants to go over the Trujillo case."

Chang is a claims supervisor at Hawaiian Indemnity. Ventura is his boss. "Which one is that?"

Frank pauses at the door. "Trujillo is a police officer on Maui. He was investigating a suspected burglary on our client's property and got hit on the head by a falling coconut. It knocked him out. He claims minor brain damage which restricts him to desk work. We represent the homeowner who was probably too cheap to have his trees trimmed."

I settled a case like that about a year ago but more tragic. A young couple took their one year old to the pool at the Hawaii Beach hotel. A coconut fell on the baby's head killing him instantly. We settled fast. I remind Frank of that case.

He responds. "This isn't that serious, but I'm going to get some authority and try to settle. You'll be pleased to hear that I'm completely prepared. I've got to go. I'm meeting Ben at Oahu. See you later. Good luck."

Finishing my lunch, I feel that if I eat one more turkey sandwich I'll start gobbling. The thought of having a leisurely lunch at the Oahu Country Club is almost beyond comprehension. Maybe tomorrow with Granger. Over the intercom, David asks if he can see me for a minute. I tell him only if he brings me a fresh cup of coffee. Two minutes later he enters with the coffee and hands me some files. They all pertain to the Andrews rape case. As I look through them he says, "We've completed the jury instructions and Dr. Bertram's deposition is scheduled for Friday afternoon. Julie has worked up a psychological profile of prospective jurors. She wants mainly men, under thirty, as they won't have too much empathy for the plaintiff. She also suggests that we try to exclude women under sixty. She says younger women would tend to identify with the plaintiff. We meet with the two security men tonight at six.

Scanning the files, I see another shot weekend ahead. Kathy is not going to be pleased. I tell David, "Make sure the court reporter delivers a copy of the deposition here on Saturday morning. What about the Ferraro case? How is that going?"

"It'll be ready to go. The deposition of Ferraro's plastic surgeon is scheduled for next Thursday afternoon. We'll work on jury instructions Monday and get you a memo on the new dog bite laws in Hawaii. Can we settle it?"

I ask, "Who's representing the plaintiff?"

"Warren Klein. He was with a trial firm in Seattle. Works for the Crown firm. Seems competent."

I nod. The Crown firm is one of the best in Hawaii. "Let me talk to Ventura and see what he thinks, but if I remember right they wanted too much." I get up to leave. "I've got to get back to court. Closing arguments start in twenty minutes."

David wishes me good luck as I walk out the door. I've never felt as confident about an outcome of a case as I feel about this one. It's a result of my painstaking preparation combined with Ing's negligence and his client's prevaricating. I'm certain that Daniels lied to Ing. A cardinal rule is never lie to your lawyer. My closing argument will be the coup de grace, but the Daniels case is already in its death throes.

As I enter the courtroom and approach the counsel table, Mrs. Lee welcomes me with a grateful smile. She may not be as confident as I am, but her anxiety seems to have all but vanished. Ing and his client look depressed, like they're going to be placed in a barrel and shoved over Niagara Falls.

It's all over before six, and I'm back in the office telling Frank and David about it.

"How long was the jury out?" Frank asks.

Leaning back in my chair, I can't help chuckling a little as I reply, "Thirty minutes and they probably spent twenty picking a foreman. In my argument, I admitted negligence but hit hard on causation. There was no way they could find that this accident was the cause of any of his alleged injuries."

Frank said, "Congratulations. I can't remember the last time I heard of a defense verdict in a rear end collision."

I smile, "It doesn't happen too often but this was an unusual situation. Daniels was one of the biggest liars I've ever seen. By the way, while waiting for the verdict I had a chance to talk to Sakumoto's law clerk. He expressed an interest in joining our firm. He seems very bright and is interested in doing trial work. Also, he's a nice guy. Do either of you know him?"

Frank nods. "Yes. I think his name is Sidney Morikami. I've talked to him several times. One good thing is that he's local."

I agree with Frank and say, "I asked him to send us a resume. He said he would and I think he would fit in."

David smiles. "You mean he wouldn't mind putting in twenty-four hours a day, seven days a week. He must be as crazy as the rest of us."

We're interrupted by the intercom announcing that two gentlemen from the Beach Hotel have been directed to our conference room. David and I go to join them.

Entering the conference room, we greet the two security officers from the hotel. Dennis Engle is director of security for the hotel chain which is comprised of six hotels in Waikiki. Jim Valdez is head of security for the Beach Hotel where the rape occurred. I'm very familiar with Valdez as he's testified in a number of cases which I've handled on behalf of his hotel. He's always been a good witness – truthful, honest and sincere. I've only met Engle on one or two occasions and have no experience with him as a witness.

The two men are nothing alike. Engle is short and scrawny with shifty eyes that refuse to look directly into mine. He looks like he hasn't had a decent meal in days. He's wearing a faded aloha shirt which appears as if it was picked up at a fire sale. It sits over pants which, I'm positive, have never been ironed.

In contrast, Valdez is over six feet tall, well built and extremely good looking with thick black hair and large brown eyes which seem to miss nothing around him. A former Navy boxing champion, he obviously continues to work out on a regular basis. He's wearing a light beige shirt with 'Beach Hotel' embroidered over the left breast pocket, tucked into clean, well ironed khaki pants. Compared to Valdez, Engle gives the appearance of being a homeless derelict. Yet, Engle is Valdez's boss. Go figure.

I ask Valdez about his knowledge of previous incidents involving entries by way of lanai doors, but Engle breaks in and starts talking about basic security procedures at the hotel chain.

David rolls his eyes letting me know that we're in trouble. I nod in agreement, thinking that this is going to be a very long night.

CHAPTER 12

It's Thursday noon and I drive to the Oahu Country Club to meet Richard Granger for lunch. As I enter the dining room of the clubhouse, I look around and spot several other lawyers huddling with their clients over sandwiches.

I see Granger sitting at a corner table, holding a glass of wine and gazing through a large picture window at a breathtaking view. By day the lush fairways almost sparkle under the fierce glare of the midday sun. Downtown Honolulu, with its multi storied buildings, looks clean, almost sterile under the same sun. The ocean is a deep blue with not one boat on its vast surface. It looks like a huge, inert lake.

I greet Granger and say, "Sorry I'm late Richard. They have a good wine selection here, don't they? I'm glad you were able to order a glass." A waiter approaches and I order a glass of iced tea.

Granger is pleased about the Daniel case and tells me, "I was happy to hear the result in the Daniels case. You did a good job, as usual." He continues, "Tell me about the Andrews rape case."

He's listening closely as we discuss the case. Granger is my height but outweighs me by at least thirty pounds. A pleasant man with a sad demeanor masking a quick mind, he has a tough approach to handling claims which has been sharpened by over thirty years in the business. He was well trained at Global Insurance, parent company of First Hawaiian.

By now he has completely reviewed the file and agrees with me that it's highly unlikely anyone was able to climb up to her room by way of the lanais. Granger asks, as he takes a sip of wine, "How do the security people come across?"

Though I never drink at lunch, I look enviously at his wine as I reply, "The chief security officer for the hotel is Jim Valdez. He retired from the navy after serving twenty years with shore patrol. He's bright and will be a good witness for us. At his deposition, he testified that the hotel has never had an illegal entry through the lanai doors and, therefore, never recommended that warning decals be put on. He went through all of the security measures the hotel has in place and they certainly seem more than adequate. I think he'll be an excellent witness on behalf of the hotel. As you know, the chain consists of about six Hawaiian hotels, all of them insured by First Hawaiian."

I take a sip of my tea and continue. "The head of security for the chain is Dennis Engle who, in my opinion, is somewhat of a loose cannon." The waiter comes and I order a hamburger. Granger orders a club sandwich.

Granger nods for me to go on. "First of all," I continue, "Engle isn't too bright. Next, he's egotistical. Put these together and, to say the least, we have a very unreliable witness. He loves the sound of his own voice and never stops talking. But he's like a talking bird which makes no sense and doesn't really have any idea of what it's talking about. I have no idea how such an incompetent person could have been hired for that position."

Granger looks gloomy, "I think he's some sort of relative. Isn't there any way to keep him out of the courtroom?"

I laugh, "Not a chance, he's been subpoenaed by the plaintiff. He has to show up."

Granger takes another sip of his wine and asks, "Even though it doesn't seem likely that the rapist got in her room by climbing the lanais, the medical records confirm that she was raped. If Engle is as bad as you say, it seems to me we should settle. What do you think?"

'I'm certain the jury will believe she was raped, but if he didn't enter through the lanai door as she claims, she had to let him in. In that case there's certainly no liability on the part of the hotel. However, I agree that the case should be settled. I think she'll be a good witness on her own behalf and if Engle can't be controlled, it could be a large verdict. The problem is that her attorney says he won't settle for less than $350,000 and I think that's much too high."

Granger shakes his head, "I agree. I think the case should be settled in the $50,000 to $100,000 range. I'll give you authority for up to $100,000, but let me know if her attorney lowers his demand."

Our lunch arrives and I take a big bite out of my hamburger. My first in weeks and it's absolutely fabulous. Our discussion about the rape case is over, so I ask Granger about his family. He has a son who's been out of high school for two years and is still without a job and a daughter who, we are sure, is on drugs. No wonder he looks sad. I feel fortunate that both of my girls are doing well in college. I can thank Kathy for that.

He finishes his wine, and I gesture for the waiter to bring him another glass. He sadly shakes his head. "Both kids are driving us up a wall. Fred still doesn't have a job. Almost any claims department in town would hire him, but he says claims work is too stressful. Hell, what isn't stressful? And Helen won't communicate with us. A junior in high school and she barely utters a word in the house. My wife and I feel like complete failures as parents." He smiles, but there's only sadness in his eyes. "So much for life in paradise." He then adds, as he reaches into his briefcase and pulls out a folder, "By the way, "I have a new case for you."

Not that I need any more work, but I'm always interested in a new case and ask him what it's about.

He replies, "A 15 year old boy from Houston went through a closed glass door at the Kona Beach Hotel. His right arm was almost severed."

"Did the glass have decals on it?" I ask.

"Absolutely. We sealed off the room and took pictures of the broken glass. There were a number of decals still on it."

"Then what's the basis of his lawsuit?"

"Either that the pictures are phony, which they're not, or that the glass did not conform to code, which it did."

Driving back to my office, I again reflect on how lucky I've been with my daughters. Their mother's death and our subsequent move to Hawaii took place when they were only three and five and it was lonely for the three of us. I married Kathy five years after our move and the four of us became a family. Both of girls adore her and by now consider her their true mother. I'm certain that without her help I wouldn't have been so fortunate. I owe her a lot. And she deserves more than the attention I've been able to give her lately. She's a good woman who deserves a faithful devoted husband, and even as my thoughts stray to Elaine I have pangs of guilt.

The moment I enter my office, Marsha hands me about ten phone messages. I scan through them and see nothing earth shaking. Lawyers wanting to settle cases, claims adjustors wanting to know what's happening on their cases and an invitation for golf on Sunday. In my dreams. I look through my correspondence and see six resumes from lawyers, two new lawsuits to review, a number of requests from claims adjustors for status reports, a stack of answers to interrogatories and another stack of medical records to be reviewed. I lean back and close my eyes in a futile attempt to recharge and find enough energy to attack it all.

Having dozed off for a few moments, I'm unaware that Julie has quietly entered the room and is sitting across from me. Seeing me open my eyes, she hands me a folder marked 'Jury Instructions' for the Andrews case. I look through them quickly and tell her I'll take a closer look at them later.

She asks, "Can I bring you current on Andrews?" I nod and she continues. "The jury instructions deal mainly with the legal responsibility of a hotel for the criminal acts of third parties. Basically it's a question of whether the hotel acted reasonably in protecting its guests, warning them of potential problems, etc. Dr. Bertram is meeting with Ms. Andrews this afternoon and the plaintiff's attorney is deposing him tomorrow afternoon. If you wish, I can attend. After that I'll re-depose the plaintiff to bring us current on her damages. There's a pre-trial conference tomorrow morning at eight. The case will be ready to go on Monday morning."

I nod again, "Sounds good to me. But I want you to second chair me. You can help me with all the psychiatric mumble-jumble."

She leaves the room and I look again at the mass of papers on my desk, thinking that maybe I should go home and drown myself in my pool but remembering that it's not deep enough for that.

A voice through the intercom breaks into my reverie. "A Mr. Lui on line 6 for you, Mr. Dorsey."

I hit line 6. "Good afternoon, Bill. How are you?" Bill Lui is a thirty year old lawyer, of Chinese descent, who has a fast growing personal injury practice. This is due, in part, to his competence and outgoing personality but also, in larger part, to the advertising he does in the local Chinese newspapers.

After perfunctorily discussing the state of our health for a few moments, he asks, "Have you had a chance to see my demand letter in the Leong case?"

I think hard and then remember. We represent a driver who, while lighting a cigarette, knocked over a young bicyclist. The boy had a broken leg which has apparently healed. The insurance carrier gave me authority to settle for up to $50,000. Bill's demand is $100,000. I answer, "Yes, I have seen your letter. I've been authorized to settle for $10,000."

"He practically yells into the phone, "That's bubkes! There isn't a judge on Oahu who would approve that."

I laugh, "Where did you learn that word?"

He chuckles. "I went to N.Y.U. Law School. Yiddish is my second language. How about being a mensch and offering $80,000."

I lean back in my chair thinking that I love this part of my profession. "Can you say that in Chinese? Maybe I can talk my client into $20,000."

"I don't speak any foreign languages, only Yiddish. Mark, you've got to do better than that. After all, he was in a cast for six weeks and then went through rehab for two months. Make it $60,000 and we've got a deal."

I can tell that he really wants to settle. His clients must be pushing him. "That's true but we paid all of his medical and rehab bills and he's fine now." Under Hawaii No Fault Law, the car that strikes a bicyclist pays all medical bills. I continue. "But since you're such a linguist I'll try for $45,000. Not a dime more.

He pretends he's crying as he says. "I think I can talk my clients into that. I'll send you a court order approving our settlement." Then he laughs, "You're really a mumser."

"OK. I'll get you a check as soon as I receive court approval. By the way, what's a mumser?"

He laughs again. "You don't want to know. Goodbye." I hear a click, and he's gone. One more case I don't have to worry about.

I hang up and again look at the piles of paper on my desk. Looking out my window, I can see a large cruise ship heading out to sea. How would it feel, I wonder, sitting on its deck, sipping a cold drink with nothing to do until dinner time except watch all the pretty girls walk by.

Then Marsha bursts into the room and once again my day dreams are interrupted. "Here" she says, handing me an official looking document, "This just arrived by express. It's from the Ninth Circuit Court of Appeals in San Francisco."

My first thought is that I've been subpoenaed before a grand jury, but it's nothing that drastic. It says the Ninth Circuit will be hearing arguments in San Francisco at 10:00 AM the following Friday in the matter of Dobrinsky vs. Big Island Land Co.

My spirits rise. I can finish the Andrews case on Thursday, take the red-eye to San Francisco Thursday night, argue the case on Friday morning, spend Friday afternoon and Saturday with Elaine, have Rachel drive up from Santa Clara to join me on Saturday night and Sunday and fly back to Honolulu on Sunday evening so I can start the dog bite case on Monday morning. I tell Marsha to make the necessary reservations and I call my daughter to let her know. My next call will be to Elaine. The papers on my desk don't look nearly so formidable now.

CHAPTER 13

"What a morning!" I almost have to yell to be heard. Frank, Dave and I are having lunch at Sings. I had asked Julie to join us but she said she wanted to review the psychiatric reports and depositions one more time. The food is good, the prices are right and it's convenient, only two short blocks from the office. However, at noon, the noise level is overpowering and shouting is almost mandatory. The advantage is that no matter how loud you speak it's impossible to be overheard at the next table.

I continue between bites of Sings' special noodles, "Engle testified this morning. What an idiot! After all the preparation we went through he testified that it's very common for what he calls 'cat burglars' to climb from lanai to lanai. He went on to say because of that he advised management to put warning signs on the lanai doors."

Frank asks, "How much did the plaintiff pay him?"

Dave laughs and says with the voice of experience from his time as a prosecutor, "First of all, they're called 'cat burglars' because they're so quiet, not because they're climbers. Second, I thought there had been no prior illegal entries through lanai doors."

"I don't know if he was paid or not, but he should have been. He blew us out of the water on liability. I had to cross-examine him to get him to admit there had been no prior entries at this hotel. Jim Valdez and the manager will testify that they were never advised to put warning signs on the lanai doors. We were absolutely astounded by Engles' testimony."

"The problem," says Frank, "Is that your people are contradicting each other. Not good. Has the plaintiff testified?"

A Reasonable Person

"Yes. She was very good. Her psychiatrist testifies this afternoon, and tomorrow morning Valdez and the manager will testify. Our psychiatrist will testify tomorrow afternoon and we'll argue on Thursday. I have to catch a flight to San Francisco Thursday night."

"Damn! I hate these things," Dave says, as he tries to pick up a noodle with his chopsticks. "We use forks in New Jersey. Much more civilized. I've heard," he continues, "you're going to argue the Big Island Land Company case on Friday morning." Dave helped me with the briefs.

Frank says, "They were using chopsticks in China ages before anyone even thought of New Jersey." He then asks, "What's that case about?"

Dave answers as I shovel more noodles into my mouth. "Mr. and Mrs. Dobrinsky came to Hawaii from Reno for a vacation about two years ago. While driving around the Big Island they stopped to take a walk on property owned by Big Island Land. According to Mr. Dobrinsky, while he and his wife were standing on a cliff enjoying the sunset, the land under Mrs. Dobrinsky collapsed causing her to fall some sixty feet to her death. He's claiming our client failed to warn of the potential danger."

Frank almost chokes on his noodles. "Sounds to me like he did her in. I can't believe a jury would find for him."

Dave continues. "If there had been prior incidents an argument could be made that a warning sign should have been posted, but there were no such incidents."

I now add. "In addition, an investigation in Reno revealed that one year before her death his wife had inherited substantial property from her parents which passed to him. To add a little spice to the story, within three months after his wife died, his secretary moved in with him."

Frank smiles. "I like my original theory even better. But tell me, just in case, where exactly is that spot?"

Dave and I laugh but we both know that Frank and Lynn haven't been getting along too well. Frank is joking about something that must be troubling him.

Frank then asks, "Why the hearing before the Ninth Circuit? What happened?"

Dave answers. "Mark came up with the Recreational Use Statute which absolves a landowner of liability from anyone using their property for recreational purposes. Sightseeing falls within the definition of a recreational use. There are some exceptions but I don't think any of them apply in this case. Fortunately, Judge Pierce agreed with us and granted our motion to dismiss."

I add. "The plaintiff's lawyer has appealed to the Ninth Circuit claiming the statute is unconstitutional."

Frank asks, "Do any other states have this law? I've never heard of it."

Dave answers. "About twenty states have the same law and they've all been held valid, but this is the first to be heard by the Ninth Circuit. We're fairly certain the court will affirm Judge Pierce in this case."

Frank nods his head in agreement as we finish our lunch. Of course they both get up leaving me to pay the bill.

Frank and I walk to court, and Dave returns to the office. Frank started a trial that morning involving injuries arising out of an auto accident. I ask him how the case is going and he shrugs his shoulders indicating it's fairly routine.

I then ask. "How are you doing? You haven't seemed your normal bubbly self recently."

He smiles somewhat sadly. "I haven't been in the best of moods. Lynn and I are having some serious problems. I don't know how much longer our marriage is going to last." He then adds, "And it doesn't help that I have so little time for her. It seems like all we do is work. If we're not preparing cases for trial we're trying them. We get to the office early and don't get home until late. All I can do when I get home is have a quick drink, eat a cold dinner and go to bed."

By now we're standing in front of Kamehameha's statue. I say, "I know exactly how you feel. It's one big grind. It's too bad that it's hurting your marriage. Fortunately for me, Kathy is very understanding."

Frank looks at me and says. "Yes, Kathy is an angel, but Lynn is turning into a real bitch and I don't know what to do. Also, all she does is shop. She runs up bills that are unbelievable. She'll buy anything that has a price tag on it. All of our credit cards are maxed out and I'm still paying a small fortune in child support to my first wife."

We enter the courthouse and I suspect that he's probably already met someone else, but if he divorces Lynn it will cost him another small fortune. Outside the courtroom I see Jack Weiss, attorney for Ms. Andrews. I say hello and then, "I just spoke to my carrier and they gave me authority for $100,000.00. Can we settle?"

He laughs out loud. He has one of the ugliest laughs I've ever heard. "You've got to be kidding. Your own security chief as much as admitted liability. I should raise my demand to $500,000.00."

A Reasonable Person

Although I feel myself getting angry I tell him, "If you're willing to lower your demand to a reasonable figure let me know."

He smirks and we enter the courtroom. Sitting on our side of counsel table is Julie. She hands me a deposition. "Here's the psychiatrist's depo. I've marked the appropriate pages and underlined all of his testimony which is helpful to us."

I go through it. "Good job. I don't think he'll hurt us too much."

Julie agrees. "He says that she was fine within several months after the incident and should have no residual problems."

As we wait for the judge, I look at Weiss and he's still smirking. I look at the photos again and continue to marvel that anyone could have climbed to the ninth floor by way of the lanais. On the other hand I don't believe I can convince this jury that the plaintiff would have let a stranger enter her room. It seems to me that as a single woman alone in a hotel room, she should have locked all the doors. It's certainly arguable that a reasonable person, under those circumstances, would have done so. Also, I think I can get her psychiatrist to testify that by the end of the summer she was physically and mentally able to return to work. Apparently the trauma resulting from the rape was not as serious as she's trying to make it out to be.

I remember words spoken long ago by one of my law professors. 'If the law is on your side pound on the law. If the facts are on your side pound on the facts.' Someone asked what to do if neither the law nor the facts are on your side. He replied, 'In that case pound on the table!'

The bailiff requests all to stand and Judge Azeka enters the room. Another 442nd veteran, Judre Azeka is a no-nonsense, all-business type with an excellent legal mind. Probably the best judge in the state. However, he turned us down cold on our motion requesting the jury to view the premises. That hurt, but nothing has gone right for us in this case. It's time I started pounding on the table!

CHAPTER 14

I arrive in San Francisco early on Friday morning. By the time I rent a car, drive into the city and am finally shown to my hotel room it's almost 7:00 A.M. Fortunately, my hearing isn't until 11:00A.M. I set my travel alarm for 9:45A.M. and get a few hours sleep before taking a cab to the Ninth Circuit Court.

Though fifteen minutes early, I walk quickly through the ornate, marble lined lobby and scan the bulletin board near the elevators. The Dobrinsky case is to be heard in room 412 and I take an elevator to the fourth floor.

As I enter the courtroom, a case is being argued before the three judge panel. A young athletic looking lawyer in a navy blue suit stands confidently in front of the lectern. Before he can complete a sentence, he's hit by a machine gun like barrage of questions, all having to do with a search and seizure question in a criminal case. He tries to answer but soon they've cut him off at the knees. Next, they riddle his torso so all that's left is a talking head muttering jibberish. His time is up and he sits down, a sweating shell of his former self. I feel like getting up and sprinting out of this madhouse.

After a short recess, my case is called and Stearns and I take our respective seats. Stearns is called to argue. As he approaches the lectern, he has the forlorn look of a prisoner being taken before a firing squad. I feel that he should be offered a blindfold and last cigarette before the inquisition begins. I can't help but feel sorry for him.

One of the judges lobs a question at him. "How many times has the constitutionality of Recreational Use statutes been appealed?"

Stearn's voice quivers, "I think five times, your honor."

The judge bellows, "I count six!" He continues, "How many times has the statute been ruled unconstitutional?" Before poor Stearns can answer, the judge roars at him, "Never! So, why should we overrule the decisions of six other jurisdictions?"

Sterns starts to answer that the issue has never been decided by the Ninth Circuit, but another judge starts throwing questions at him. It doesn't take long for Stearns to be totally demolished. I now pity him as he sits down.

It's my turn. I stand before the judges, my knees shaking, not knowing what kind of bomb they're going to throw at me. I say to the court, "Your honors, I'll submit this matter on our brief. I'll do my best to answer any questions you may have."

Judge Ryan, sitting tall in his chair, may look like a kindly old grandfather, but once he puts on his black robe he turns into a deadly vampire, fangs bared, ready to suck the blood of any lawyer who dares to bring a case before him. But his voice is surprisingly mellow as he asks, "Mr. Dorsey, isn't it true that, in this case, the plaintiff and the decedent were trespassers?"

Knowing where this is going, I reply, "Yes your honor, but….."

He cuts me off in a tone that could cut through bone. "Since there's no duty on the part of a landowner to warn trespassers of potential dangers why do we have to be concerned with the constitutionality of the recreational use statute?" He looks at me like I'm a first year law student.

I try to be as succinct as possible. "Your honor, under Hawaiian law, there's no distinction between people invited on the property and trespassers. The same duty is owed to each."

In a tone of angry disbelief, he demands, "Are you saying that if a burglar enters my home and slips on some spilled milk, for instance, that I could be liable for his resulting injuries?"

I answer in a respectful tone, "Absolutely." I refrain from telling him that I lost a case exactly like that about five years ago on Maui.

I then add, "Of course your house would have to be in Hawaii." The other two judges actually smile. Ryan shakes his head and says, "I have no further questions. Neither of the other judges have any questions. At this point it seems fairly certain that they'll affirm Judge Pierce's ruling but I'm still pleased to leave the courtroom.

Up to now, I'd been focusing strictly on the case, but my thoughts return to Elaine as I return to the hotel. It's noon as I arrive at the hotel restaurant and I await her arrival with almost unbearable joy. By now, I'm ready for a stiff drink.

I ask for a booth by a window and the head waiter leads me to one with a spectacular view across the city to the Bay Bridge and beyond to Berkeley. I order a vodka martini on the rocks and Elaine appears as I take my first sip.

She stands by the table looking absolutely stunning. Her pant legs are tucked into dark brown, highly polished leather boots. She's wearing an embroidered western style shirt and a suede vest with pearl buttons. Although this looks like an outfit for an outdoors person, one look at her pale white skin is evidence that she's very seldom in the sun.

I stand, give her a hug and kiss and we sit. She orders a martini with three olives, smiles and says, "You look very distinguished in a suit, but I thought you Hawaiians wore aloha shirts."

"We do, but not in court."

The waiter hands us two menus that appear larger than the New York Times. He leaves us alone guessing correctly that we're not ready to order. I turn to Elaine and say, "You look beautiful. It looks like you're dressed for horseback riding."

She laughs, "No way, not with what this outfit costs. You look tired. I think what you need is a good massage. We should order."

I motion for the waiter and say, "I agree. I could use a nice massage, and you look very sexy. I should have saved some money and taken you right to my room."

"Don't worry. We'll be there soon enough. Besides we would have ordered from room service and that's even more expensive."

The waiter, an aging hippie with a long pony tail, asks for our order. Elaine asks if the salmon is fresh. He answers in a condescending manner, "All of our fish is fresh." She orders the salmon and he humorously asks, "In or out of the can, Ma'am?"

We all laugh and I feel compelled to ask if the halibut is fresh. He answers, "They're reeling it in as we speak."

I point to our near empty glasses and he says, "I'll bring you fresh martinis. You'll need them to help wash down the fish."

As he leaves I tell Elaine, "Nowadays, everyone's a comedian."

She laughs, "Especially in San Francisco."

Later in my room I'm lying naked on the bed. Elaine is softly rubbing my back. I ask her to massage my shoulders. "I had a tough session this morning."

"Poor baby," she says, as her hands start squeezing my shoulders. "Is that better? How are your girls?"

It feels wonderful and I tell her so. "They're doing well, thank you. Rachel is still at Santa Clara. She started her junior year and is thinking of law school. I'm going to try and talk her out of it. A little harder, please."

She squeezes my shoulders until they hurt. "That's better. Rose started U.C. San Diego. She's in pre-med, wants to be a pediatrician. How are your kids?"

"They're also doing well, thanks. My oldest son graduated from the University of Colorado receiving a degree in downhill skiing. My second son is starting college and my daughter is in high school." Her hands move down to my butt.

As she rubs, I start to get excited. She tells me to roll over. I tell her, "That could be embarrassing unless you take your clothes off too."

Later we're both lying naked on the bed. She asks, "How did you like the massage?"

"The massage was great but what came after was much better."

She laughs, "For me, too. But tell me, how are you getting along with your wife?"

This is the first time she has ever asked this. I answer, "Actually, we get along very well. She's the only woman I know who can put up with me. Why do you ask?"

She lights a cigarette. "I'm not getting along very well with Jack. We seem to argue most of the time. He's really becoming a pain in the ass."

I smile, "I thought you were the pain in the ass. I told you not to marry him."

She takes a long drag and says, "You did not! You had to go away to college and law school leaving me all alone. I asked you not to leave. You could have gone to a school close to home."

Remembering that we've had this discussion a dozen times, I say, "No, I couldn't get scholarships to any colleges close to home. And, I asked you to wait. You said you'd wait forever."

She looks sad, "I waited for more than two years. At the time it seemed forever."

"Then you met Jack. I wrote you a letter begging you not to marry him."

"I never received that letter. But I probably would have married him anyway." She puts out her cigarette, kisses my stomach and says, "I know it was a mistake." Her mouth goes lower, "Hmm, what have we here? Looks like someone is ready again."

She leaves at five and I lie on the bed, close my eyes and immediately fall asleep. In my dreams I hear a telephone buzzing. It's no dream. I turn on the light and see by the bedside clock that it's a few minutes after nine. Six in Honolulu. I pick up the phone. "Hello."

A voice answers. It's Julie. "Hello. Mark, is that you?"

"Yes, Julie, what is it?"

"The jury returned a verdict in the rape case. They found for the plaintiff and awarded her $100,000."

My heart sinks. "That's exactly what we offered."

"Yes, but they found she was also negligent for not locking the lanai door. I spoke to the foreman after the verdict. He told me that her admission to you, under cross examination, that she simply forgot to lock it led to their decision. They deducted 45% for her negligence for a net award of $55,000."

I feel better but I'll never understand juries. "That's great. I couldn't have done it without your help. Thanks."

"You're welcome. We bought some champagne and are going to drink a toast to you. Go back to whatever you were doing."

"OK. Thanks again." We hang up and I turn over and am soon in a dreamless sleep.

The following day Elaine comes directly to my room and we order from room service. Two cheeseburgers, fries, two straight up martinis for Elaine and a double martini on the rocks for me. I could easily get used to this lifestyle.

Later, we're lying on the bed. I kiss her on the lips. "That was fantastic. You're fantastic."

She laughs, "So are you. I guess we're just good together." She turns on her back, lights a cigarette and says, "I have to talk to you about something."

I see her mood has changed. "What is it?"

"I'm seriously thinking of leaving my husband. Our marriage is becoming a joke. He's mean, selfish and uncaring."

I ask, "Why are you telling me this." As soon as the words are out I realize it's a very dumb question.

She sits up and waves her hand in front of my face. "Hel-low. Remember, I love you, you love me. I leave my husband, you leave your wife. We get married and live happily forever after"

I practically gulp. "When do you think this will happen?"

Again my response is obviously not what she wants to hear. She looks at me as though wondering if I'm being deliberately obtuse, and I can see that she's almost in tears. Then she explains what she has in mind. "It can't be right away. He makes good money, but we're terribly in debt. All we own is our house and that's mortgaged to the hilt. His business does well, but he's a big gambler. I told him that if he doesn't stop gambling and get us out of debt I'm going to leave him."

I reflect for a moment, "So, what you're saying is that when he stops gambling and gets out of debt you'll leave him."

She smiles. "Yes. It's always been tough to pull the ool over your eyes."

I turn on my back. I've got to think. The first question that enters my mind is whether I can leave Kathy. She's been a wonderful, caring wife and, though it's not with the same passion I feel for Elaine, I do love her.

Next, I think of my finances. I'm doing well but with high mortgage payments and two girls in college there isn't much left over.

And, can I leave Frank in the lurch? He's a terrible businessman and the firm needs to be expanded to take care of all the business that keeps pouring in. That means hiring more lawyers, para-legals and secretaries. On top of that, we're entering the computer age which means thousands of dollars into computers. I'm not sure Frank is capable of handling all of that on his own.

Never before have I felt so damn confused.

Elaine looks at me and asks, "What are you thinking?"

I roll over on top of her. "I'll show you." This is the response she wants, one that reassures her that I'm in her power. She knows that at least for now, nothing else matters to me.

Chapter 15

It's the following Thursday evening and the jury is out on the Ferraro dog bite case. Frank and I are alone in his office. It's not as large as mine but is a corner room with a view of the mountains from one set of windows and the ocean from the other. He closes the door, brings out a bottle of brandy and two glasses, pours us each a healthy amount and then asks, "How did it go?"

I'm still thinking of Elaine, "How did what go?"

"The trial. What else?"

I take a sip of the brandy. Though I'm no judge of brandies, it's obvious that this is exceptional. I answer his question, "Not bad. There was a big sign on the fence warning people about the dog. Nevertheless, she stuck her head over the gate and yelled for the occupant. No one was home as both were at work. The injuries were bad. Pictures of her face taken at the hospital were gruesome. But her plastic surgeon did a great job, and she looks pretty good now. This is great brandy. Where did you buy it?"

Frank also takes a sip. "Pretty good stuff. I picked it up in London. Did you object to the pictures?"

I take another sip. I still can't figure out how every time he gets a few days off he flies to London or Spain or Paris. I can't seem to find the time to do it, and his caseload is certainly equal to mine. Perhaps I'm too obsessive about my cases, but I just can't seem to help it. "You're right. It's very good, even for a beer drinker like me. No, I felt that the judge would allow them in and actually the comparison between those pictures and the way she looks now is incredible and I think favorable to the defense."

"What do you think the jury will do?"

I smile. "Up until my last question I thought it was a tossup. But my last question was completely off the wall and I had no idea what the answer would be. I asked her where her dog was now. She started crying and said she had to put him to sleep. I thought the jury was also going to break into tears." I add gratuitously, "Of course, through a skillful use of peremptory challenges there are seven dog owners on the jury."

Frank exclaims, "What a clever question. Was he put to sleep because of this incident?"

My thoughts go back to Elaine and the inane question I asked her. I only wish I could ask such clever questions outside of courtrooms. "No, they told me later that this was his first and last bite. He basically died of old age. Not to change the subject but how are things going with you and Lynn?"

Frank pours some more brandy for both of us. "Not too good. I'll probably move out this weekend."

I take a close look at him. He looks tired and older than his thirty-nine years. He's beginning to have a hint of gray in his jet black hair. We sit in silence for awhile sipping our brandy. I feel a sudden urge to get home to Kathy. Since returning from San Francisco, I haven't spent much time with her and the least I can do after my time with Elaine is to try to make up for it by giving her some of the attention she deserves. I say to Frank, "I'm really sorry. We all like Lynn but you have to do what's best for you. Do you want to take some time off?"

"I'm trying to settle some cases and, if so, I'll see.

"I know what you mean, I have trials scheduled every week for the next year. By the way, I'm really tired. Would you mind waiting here for an hour or so. If the jury comes back you can take the verdict."

"I'll gladly wait. Are any of the associates here?"

"No, they've all gone home. They're a lot smarter than us."

He's still laughing as I leave.

Driving home the traffic is amazingly light, so I actually arrive at a decent hour. Kathy's in the kitchen, a glass of white wine in one hand, stirring a pot of pasta sauce with the other. I kiss her on the cheek and ask if there's any wine left. She nods towards the counter and I pour myself a glass, take off my jacket and sit.

She asks, "How did the trial go?"

"OK, we finished today. I asked Frank to take the verdict. I guess you heard the news."

She grimaces, "Yes, Lynn was crying on my shoulder all day. She's certain Frank has met someone else."

I don't reply and she asks, "Are you hungry?"

I smile, "Not for food. I've hardly seen you since I got back from San Francisco."

She grins, "Sounds good to me." She turns off the stove, heads for the bedroom and says over her shoulder, "We can eat later."

It's later and we're sitting at the kitchen table with large plates of pasta and two slices of garlic toast in front of us. I'm wearing an aged pair of shorts and Kathy is looking very sexy with nothing on but her old robe. She asks, "Do you have another trial next week?"

I put a forkful of pasta in my mouth and say, "Yes, it starts Monday. Odd case. A woman in her fifties was boiling water for tea on her stove in her condo in Waikiki. The stove is under a kitchen window which blew in and knocked over the tea pot causing the hot water to spill on her. She had burns on her thigh and she says on her vagina." I shovel in more pasta.

Kathy gasps, "Gee! That must have hurt."

"I'm sure it did. She went to emergency and then saw her gynecologist who referred her to a psychologist."

Kathy takes a sip of wine and asks, "Why a psychologist?"

I also take a sip, "The burns healed up fairly quickly but she claims she hasn't been able to have orgasms since the incident. Her gynecologist found no physical basis for her claim."

Kathy laughs. "Is she married?"

"No, she's divorced and living alone. But why do you ask? Is it because only married women have orgasms or because most married women don't have orgasms?" I also laugh. "Present company excluded of course."

Kathy smiles. "If it were me I'd want lots of money. How much is she asking?"

I smile. "If it were you I'd ask for lots of money too. Actually she's asking for $50,000 which I think is quite a bit. She's represented by John McDowell."

Kathy takes a very small bite of her pasta. I've finished mine and go back to the wine with a slice of garlic toast. She says, "John's such a nice guy. I really like him and his wife. Whom do you represent?"

I pour some more wine for us. "There are seven defendants including the architect, developer, general contractor, glass company, the homeowners' association and a couple more. I started out representing the general contractor but now I represent all of them."

She takes another miniscule bite of pasta and asks, "How come?"

"All of the various claims people met and decided that since liability wasn't really an issue and since the potential damages aren't too high that they would use only one lawyer to represent all of the defendants. Since I represent the general contractor they selected me. They'll divide my fee plus any settlement or judgment equally."

Kathy now takes a tiny bite of her garlic toast. "Good choice. Has there been a settlement offer?"

"Yes. They decided to offer seven thousand, one thousand each on a take it or leave it basis. John won't come off his demand so we start trial on Monday. Since liability is admitted it should be fairly quick."

Kathy pushes her plate of pasta away. More than half remains and I pull it towards me. My plate is empty and I'm still hungry. She says, "Be careful. You'll gain weight and I don't like fat men."

I push the plate away and say, "I haven't had a chance to tell you about my visit with Rachel."

"Please tell me all about it."

"It was wonderful. She came to San Francisco on Saturday afternoon and we had a great seafood dinner at Scomas. She's turning into a real beauty. Every guy in the place was probably wondering what such a pretty young thing was doing with an old fart like me."

Kathy laughs and throws me a compliment, "They probably thought you were her boyfriend. You don't look old enough to be her father."

"Thank you, but I doubt that. Anyway, it was the best abalone I've ever had. We then returned to the hotel and had a drink at their bar. My room had two big double beds so I didn't have to get her a separate room. The next morning we took a cable car to the wharves and had breakfast at The Vista with their famous Irish coffee. We then played tourists, walking around, going in and out of the shops. I bought her some clothes and a funny looking hat she wanted. We then had a late lunch, took the cable car back to the hotel and off she went. It was a fun visit."

Kathy asks, "Did she say anything about school?"

"Yes, she loves it and she's made a lot of friends. No serious boyfriends but she's dating a few that she likes."

"Wonderful. Too bad Rose couldn't have come up too."

I nod. "I know but San Diego is a fairly long drive."

Kathy yawns. "I don't know about you but I'm tired. The dishes can wait till tomorrow."

I say to her, "I hope you're not too tired. This old fart still has some life in him."

She smiles as she takes my hand and leads me into the bedroom.

I'm a lucky man. Kathy is, as Frank said, an angel, everything a man could want a wife to be – attractive, supportive, interesting, a lover and a friend. If she knew what I had done in San Francisco, she would be devastated. And it would be terribly painful now if she knew how my thoughts were straying even as we made love. I realize even that type of betrayal is unforgiveable.

CHAPTER 16

It's ten the next morning and I'm sitting in the coffee room finishing my third cup and almost ready for another. I'm still savoring the pleasure of last night. I find it difficult leading a double life. Sometimes I wonder who I'm being faithful or unfaithful to. I don't have a clue as to what my next step will be. I know that I should tell Elaine that we have to stop seeing each other, as infrequent as it may be. But I don't seem able to bring myself to do that. I'm bound to her like a man possessed. The situation is beginning to tear me apart.

Frank bursts into the room like an exploding hand grenade, followed by David and Julie. Frank says to them, "Did you hear? Mark got a defense verdict in the doggie case. He had to kill the dog to do it, but it was probably worth it. Besides it was no puppy."

We're all smiling as they pour their coffee and David says, "I took a couple of depositions in that case, it was a real dog."

Julie adds, "I agree. That woman had no business sticking her head over the gate, especially when there was a 'Beware Of Dog' sign as plain as day. There's no strict liability for a dog owner in Hawaii."

Somewhat defensively, I say, "True. But also in Hawaii it doesn't matter whether the dog has bitten anyone before or not. The question, under our dog-bite law, is whether the plaintiff actually entered the premises by looking over the fence and, if so, whether such entry was a lawful one. The jury found that she had entered without being invited. Accordingly, it wasn't a lawful entry, the warning sign was on the fence, thus no liability."

Frank interjects, "What's up for next week?"

David volunteers, "The Whitton case." He explains the case to Frank and Julie.

Frank laughs, "Oh, the case of the missing orgasm."

David shakes his head. "No, we call it the case of the burnt pussy."

All but Julie are laughing. Frank then turns to her and asks, "How much would you ask for if you couldn't have orgasms for the rest of your life?"

David and I manage to keep straight faces as Julie turns red, stands up and says to Frank, "Fuck you!" and storms out of the room.

My annoyance is obvious as I say to Frank, "In some states you could be sued for saying that."

Frank replies, "Not in Hawaii. Not yet."

I'm still irritated, "It doesn't matter. You shouldn't speak that way to employees."

David turns to Frank, "Don't you think that was hitting below the belt?"

At that we all smile and I ask David to come to my office so we can discuss the Whitton case. Marsha has placed a brown folder on my desk with a tab reading 'Whitton v. Bancroft Towers.' I open it and see two very thin looking folders inside. Dave enters and I ask, "Is this all? There must be more."

Dave frowns, "I'm afraid not. This was another one of Andy's files and not too much was done. He took the depositions of the plaintiff and her gynecologist and got the records from her psychologist and that was it."

As I look through the file, I say, "We haven't had an independent medical exam, we haven't named a doctor, we didn't take the deposition of her psychologist. Where did he get his law degree? From Sears?"

David smiles ruefully and replies, I know. It's not too good. I tried to name a doctor of our choice and asked for an exam but Judge Camara said it was too late."

"Oh no!" I almost yell. "Not him." Camara is the most plaintiff oriented judge on the bench. He hates insurance companies and insurance defense lawyers with a passion and dislikes me in particular intensely. In private practice he represented plaintiffs and handled each case with a vengeance. He imagined that every insurance carrier and their attorneys in general and Frank and I in particular were out to sabotage all of his efforts on behalf of clients. His loathing and mistrust have followed him to the bench.

I put the file away. "I'll take this home and look at it over the weekend. Will you prepare the jury instructions? We only need standard instructions on damages since we've admitted liability." Then I ask, "What's on for the following week?" Not another of Andys I hope."

"No, Julie and I worked on it. It's the one where the kid fell out of the back of a pickup truck and under the wheel of a tour bus. His leg was crushed."

I nod. "Yes, I remember that case. Ask Julie to come in and I'll get another cup of coffee. I go back to the coffee room. Frank is still there telling a paralegal and two secretaries about the movie he saw the night before. They're all laughing. I pour myself a fresh cup and walk out without saying anything, thinking that I have to find out what's coming up on his calendar.

I return to my office, and sitting there are David and a dejected looking Julie with a big folder on her lap. She doesn't look at me as she says, "Dave said you wanted to see me on the tour bus case."

I reply, "Yes. But first I want to apologize for Frank's remark. I'm really sorry. It was completely out of line. I'm going to have a talk with him and I promise you that it won't happen again."

She looks up and gazes directly into my eyes. "I appreciate what you're saying, but the next time it happens I'm out of here. I think it was completely uncalled for."

Thinking to myself that I'd love to strangle Frank, I say, "We certainly don't want to lose you. I can assure you that we will not tolerate that type of behavior. Now, may we please discuss the tour bus case."

CHAPTER 17

Monday morning is not starting well. The moment I enter his chambers, Judge Camara starts shouting at me. He claims my offer is ridiculously low. When I suggest that the $50,000 demand is ridiculously high, he actually screams at me. "I've read the file and seen the pictures. This poor woman was seriously burned and now has a permanent dysfunction. The jury should easily award $50,000 and maybe more."

I feel like telling him that he's full of crap but the thought of spending a few days in jail makes me hold back. Instead I play the toady. "Sorry, judge, but $7,000 is all they authorized me to offer. I can't get authority for more." Unusual as it may be, I'm actually telling the truth.

John McDowell looks at me sympathetically. We've been friends for years, and he has no use for Camara either. He knows that $50,000 is substantially higher than the case is worth but has no control whatsoever over his client. He says to the judge, "Sorry, your honor, but my client is holding out for $50,000. I can't convince her to take any less."

Judge Camara turns to John and in a lower tone says, "I'm not blaming you, John. I don't think Mr. Dorsey is really interested in settling. Not with his hourly rates. I guess we have no choice but to go to trial." He turns back to me as I get up to re-enter the courtroom, "I don't want any funny business from you during this trial. I swear that if there is, I'll hold you in contempt without thinking twice about it."

Back in the courtroom I tell John, "I don't think he's capable of thinking twice."

John smiles, "I don't think he's capable of thinking at all. I have a feeling that we're in for a miserable few days."

"I agree, but at least he's being nice to you."

John shakes his head, "That's even worse. If he keeps this up the jury will have more sympathy for you than for my client. I'm already feeling sorry for you. How about you and Kathy having dinner with Joan and me tonight? My treat."

"That's the best offer I've had today. At the first break I'll call Kathy and let her know."

After selecting a jury and making opening statements, Camara dismisses us for the noon recess. I return to my office and Julie enters behind me. She asks, "How did it go?"

"Not well," I reply. "The judge was out to make my day miserable. But we'll take it as it comes." I don't feel like saying anything more about it, so I ask Julie, "Have you done what we discussed on the tour bus case?"

Marsha enters and sets a cup of coffee and a turkey sandwich in front of me along with a fistful of messages. She rushes out before I can thank her. Maybe she has a hot lunch date, but I doubt it. She seems irritated about something.

Julie smiles, "She's sure in a hurry. I hope nothing's wrong." Then, answering my question, "Yes, everything has been taken care of. I've completely reviewed the file. On the liability issue, we have the depositions of the plaintiff, bus driver, driver and other passenger of the pickup truck and the investigating police officers. There are no other eye witnesses. As far as damages, we have deposed all of the treating doctors and had Dr. Tam examine his leg. The leg was crushed and barely saved. It's a very serious injury. He'll limp for the rest of his life."

"What a shame. How old is he?"

She nods her head, "He's only nineteen. Just a kid."

I ask, "Was it determined whether it was the front or rear wheel that ran over him? If I remember right, the plaintiff's attorney claims that the kid fell in front of the bus so the driver could have avoided him."

She shakes her head. "Absolutely not. All witnesses state or infer that he fell under the back wheel."

I take a bite of my sandwich, sit back and mull it over. Julie patiently sits, scanning the files to see if anything has been overlooked. I don't think so. Still, something seems absent. Finally it hits me and I say, "The problem is that there are very serious injuries but questionable liability. Any jury would be very sympathetic in this situation. If we could separate liability from damages so the jury doesn't hear all of the medical testimony we might have a better chance at a defense verdict. Who's the judge?"

She looks up. "Sakumoto. Are you thinking we should file a motion to bifurcate?"

I smile. "Absolutely. And, knowing Judge Sakumoto, he'll be more than pleased to bifurcate the trial. The shorter the trial, the quicker he can get to his golf."

Back in the courtroom I look over the jury. I wanted a young jury consisting mainly of men. It took all of my peremptory challenges, but there are eight men and not one juror looks over 35. I'm pleased until Camara enters with his habitual scowl.

Mrs. Whitton, the plaintiff, takes the stand. She's a homely, matronly looking woman in her late fifties. She's shown some pictures of her initial burns which show some redness on her thighs. Recent photos aren't too bad. She testifies as to the pain the burns caused, her doctor visits and being referred to a psychologist. She further testifies that since the incident she's been unable to achieve an orgasm so that sex is no longer pleasurable to her. On cross examination, she testifies that she's been divorced for over nine years, since then she's had several intimate relationships, but none serious for about three years. When questioned about the psychological sessions, she says that she only went twice as she didn't think they were helping. Her testimony takes most of the afternoon and Camara recesses for the day.

Returning to my office, I feel like I've been put though a wringer. My shirt is soaking wet. What a day! On my desk is a draft copy of a motion to bifurcate in the tour bus case. It looks good. Julie does excellent work.

Marsha enters the room and asks if she can talk to me. I nod my head and she closes the door behind her. She sits and says, "I want you to know that I interviewed for another job today."

My heart sinks. The day seems to be getting worse. "Are you taking it?"

She shakes her head. "No, but you're going to have to talk to Frank."

I feel relieved but wonder what the hell Frank has done now. I ask, "What do you want me to talk to him about?"

"His mouth. He's very personable but he's got a big mouth and maybe he doesn't realize it, but he hurts peoples' feelings. He's been taking out his anger on every female in this office. I was this close to leaving." She places her thumb and forefinger so close together that there's little space between them.

"Marsha, I appreciate your giving me a chance to try to correct the situation. I really need you around here. I want you to know though that Frank is going through a very difficult time right now."

"She nods, Yes, I know that he's going through a separation but that's no excuse for his behavior."

I agree and she leaves for the night. Shit! It's always something else around here. If it's not being beaten over the head by incompetent judges, it's the intense stress I'm put through at the office. I keep hoping that Frank will help relieve me of some of the daily problems and pressures that are inherent in running a law office, but, instead, he continually adds to them. Leaning back I close my eyes, and daydream of how nice it would be if I could break out of here.

Chapter 18

It's the following morning and I'm standing outside of Camara's courtroom. John approaches and says, "I guess we're in for another miserable day."

I laugh, "Thanks again for the dinner. Excellent restaurant, great food and better company. Kathy and I had a wonderful time. But John, I really think you should convince your client to accept the $7000. I don't think this jury will award her that much."

He nods in agreement. "I've tried talking to her but its no use. She's very stubborn. She refuses to take a dime less than $50,000."

I shake my head. "That's too bad. She's not very attractive, she wasn't that seriously injured and she refuses to continue therapy with her psychologist. Plus, do you really think this jury cares if she can have an orgasm?"

John laughs. "I don't think so. I certainly don't care, that's for sure."

"Me either. "We're both laughing now. "Lets go in and face the ogre."

The rest of the morning is not too bad. Her gynecologist testifies that there was little or no damage done to her vagina. Under cross, he admits that her burns healed with no scarring or unsightly aftermath. Her psychologist says that with a few more treatments she would have been fine, but she quit treatments for no apparent reason.

John rests his case and I see no reason to call any witnesses so I also rest. Another very quick trial. We're ordered to return at 1:00PM to settle instructions and the jury is ordered to return at 2:00PM to listen to final arguments.

I walk down the block to a café and order a plate lunch of shoyu chicken with two scoops of rice to go. I take it back to the courtroom and eat while looking over the jury instructions. Mainly standard on damages since

A Reasonable Person

liability is not an issue. My mind wanders back to Elaine. I wonder whether she'll ever leave her husband. Deep down I doubt it. But, I wonder, what if she does leave him? Do we continue going on like we have been or would she expect me to leave Kathy? I recall the scenario she spelled out when we were in bed: "Remember, I love you, you love me. I leave my husband, you leave your wife. We get married and live happily forever after." I wonder what life with her would be like. Though the infrequent times we spend together are magical, how much of the magic would remain in an ongoing day-to-day relationship? Would she be willing to put up with the frequent neglect that goes with being the wife of a trial lawyer. Would I have to find a job with a law firm that does no trial work?

Time passes quickly and John returns. We're called into chambers and Camara is in a better mood. We easily settle instructions and return to the courtroom where the jurors are now returning. The judge takes his seat and we give our closing arguments. John is forced by his client to ask the jury for $50,000. A figure that is so unreasonable the jury has to ignore it. I suggest that $2,500 is more appropriate. Probably too low.

I return to my office and again attack the pile of papers on my desk. When I come up for air it's almost six. I call Kathy and tell her I won't get home until seven and walk into Frank's office. He's on the phone, motions for me to sit and finishes his conversation. It's obviously with his new girlfriend. He hangs up and asks if I want some port. He tells me he picked it up in Madrid. By now, I'm beginning to resent his jaunts to foreign countries.

I nod and he pours two drinks of the good stuff. He raises his glass and says, "Happy anniversary."

I raise my glass and say, "What the hell are you talking about? It's not my anniversary."

He smiles. "No, it's our anniversary. We got together ten years ago today."

I shake my head. "Really? Are you sure? I honestly don't remember."

"Absolutely. I mark it on my calendar every year."

I raise my glass and say, "Well then, in that case, happy anniversary. I think that everything considered it's been a good partnership. What do you think?"

He sips his brandy. "I agree, even though I was second choice."

"Now what the hell are you talking about?"

He takes another sip. "You know that this is a fairly small legal community and it got around that you had applied for a position with the Goldsmith firm. They apparently turned you down and you then took me on."

The Goldsmith firm is the largest and most prestigious firm in Hawaii with branches in Guam, San Francisco and even Washington, D.C. I look at Frank and say, "I never applied for a position with Goldsmith. Is this something that's been bothering you for ten years?"

Frank replies, "Absolutely. No one enjoys being second, especially me. And, everyone knew about your lunch with their two senior partners at the Pacific Club."

I laugh and take a sip of my port. "It's true, I did have lunch with them. But I wasn't applying for a job."

"Then what? A case? You certainly weren't discussing some rear end collision with those guys."

I smile and take another sip. "Hardly. I don't think either of them has ever seen the inside of a courtroom. As a matter of fact, they called me out of the blue, invited me to lunch and asked me to join their firm as partner in charge of their litigation department. They mentioned a large salary, car, medical and other perks. I told them I would think it over, discuss it with my wife and get back to them within a few days. I called them the next day and declined their offer."

Franks mouth falls open. "You turned down being head of the litigation department for one of the most prestigious firms in the United States? Were you crazy? You would have been great at that job."

"I don't think so. I'm not very good with large firms. They're too structured for me. Too many big bosses."

Frank actually looks puzzled. "Tell the truth. Why did you really turn it down?"

I look him straight in the eye. "That afternoon, after lunch, you came to see me about a position. You told me the lawyers you were with were breaking up and you heard that I needed another trial lawyer. I had asked around about you and everyone I spoke to said you were an excellent trial lawyer. We talked for about an hour and I was very impressed. That night I had a long talk with Kathy about what I should do and she agreed with me that since I liked you so much that I should not go with Goldsmith but, instead, put you on as a junior partner and together we should do very well. The rest is history."

I see tears in Frank's eyes. He gets up, comes around the desk, lifts me out of my chair and almost strangles me in a bear hug. I hug him back and after a few moments say, "We'd better break this up. Someone may come in and get the wrong idea."

Frank grins, returns to his chair and finishes his port. "I don't know what to say. Imagine that! Me not knowing what to say! By the way, did you come in for anything in particular?"

I finish my port and put the glass down. "Yes, I came in to tell you that you're fired."

He laughs. "I've told you a dozen times, you can't fire me. I'm a partner."

"Then damn it! Act like one and not like some college fraternity boy. First it was Julie and now Marsha. Frank, you've got to watch your big mouth. I don't want to lose either one of them."

Frank actually looks contrite. "Okay, you're right as usual. I promise I'll be more careful. I'll apologize to both of them."

"Good. One more thing. I know you've been stressed out. I looked at your schedule and your cases set for next week have all settled. How would you like to go to New York for a week?"

He brightens up. "Absolutely. I love New York. What have you got?"

"I'm handling a case for the Mana Kai hotel on Maui. One of their guests went for a swim, got knocked down by a wave and is now a paraplegic. He's from New York and I've scheduled a number of depositions. I'll be in trial next week so I can't go. I was going to send David, but since your calendar is clear it would be better if you go."

He nods. "Of course. I'd love to get away for a week. I'll get the file from Marsha." It's not hard to guess that he plans to take his girlfriend with him.

I get up. "Would you mind taking my verdict. I'm really tired."

He says as I walk out, "No problem. I'll be here for awhile. I have no home to go to."

An hour later Frank calls. "Congratulations. The verdict was for four thousand. Another victory."

"Thanks. How did John take it?"

"We're having a drink now. He says he's just glad it's over and hopes he never sees his client again."

I laugh and tell Kathy the news as we finish our dinner. She says, "There's a bottle of champagne in the fridge. We should open it and have a little celebration."

Of course, I agree.

Chapter 19

Another Monday, another trial. The jury has been selected and the plaintiff is on the witness stand. He's a very scared nineteen year old. He walked from the counsel table with an overly exaggerated limp which I'm certain was staged by his attorney. His limp has become more and more pronounced since the granting of our motion to bifurcate. It's difficult not to feel sorry for him, only a teenager when thrown under the wheels of a huge tour bus. Now he'll have a deformed leg for the rest of his life, and it's my job to see that he limps out of the courthouse with nothing.

On top of everything else, the poor kid is almost illiterate. He's of a mixed racial background, including Hawaiian, Chinese, Caucasian and who knows what else thrown in. His school record is deplorable. He barely finished the ninth grade and then dropped out of high school. It's clear that his only vocation would be manual labor at minimal wage jobs. Meanwhile, Quinn continues to drone on with his bland questions. Every time he gets close to a question involving pain, treatment, rehabilitation or medications I object on the grounds that such questions are to be reserved for the second phase of the trial. Sakumoto sustains all of my objections and Quinn is almost in shock as he realizes he has no more questions to ask.

My main thrust on cross is to show that he fell under the rear wheels of the bus or, at least, that he cannot say for sure which of the wheels ran over him. At his deposition he testified that he couldn't remember anything that happened after he fell. He now testifies that the pick up was proceeding on Beretania street in the left turn lane. The bus was on their right in the adjacent left turn lane. Suddenly the truck sped up, apparently to make the signal, and then made a very fast left turn. Although he was holding on to the side of the truck he was thrown out. He further testifies that the truck was alongside the bus which was also making a left turn. I ask him if he can describe the driver of the bus and he says, "No, all I saw was the back of his head as it went by." Since it's now obvious that he fell under the rear wheels I see no need to ask him any further questions.

The rest of the day goes smoothly. The afternoon is taken up by the driver and front seat passengers of the pickup truck. Sakumoto dismisses us early probably so he can, at least, get in nine holes. The first day of trial went well.

It's now Tuesday morning and Quinn calls the tour bus driver to the stand. His testimony has no surprises. He says that if the boy had fallen in front of the bus that he would have seen him. However, he never did see him, so there was no chance to avoid the accident. It should be a directed verdict but I know Sakumoto would never go for that.

After lunch the investigating police officers testify. Their testimony does nothing to help the plaintiff's case. We'll settle instructions and give our closing arguments the following morning.

I return to my office and settle in with a large glass of ice water. Julie enters with a file.

I tell her to sit and ask, "What's up?"

She replies, "It's really quiet around here with Frank gone. By the way, we had a nice talk before he left and he apologized."

"Good. What's that file you're holding."

She hands it to me and says, "The Thomas case. He was the retired pathologist who killed himself."

I look at her and smile. "Yes, I remember this one. His wife died when he was sixty-five so after about a year he found a new wife in some bar in Waikiki. He left her his home and half of his estate. We're representing her under their homeowners insurance."

Julie nods. "That's right. She was young enough to be his granddaughter. He was in the process of killing himself when she walked in and saw him. The plaintiffs' theory is that she was negligent in not doing anything to stop him."

I let out a grunt. "That's ridiculous! First of all she had no idea he was trying to kill himself. She thought he was shooting up which apparently was not unusual. As I recall, she even went downstairs to tell his daughter that he was shooting up. Second, even if she knew, I don't think she had a legal duty to do anything. And, finally, what could she have done to stop him?"

Julie smiles, "That's right. She did think he was shooting up and ran downstairs to tell his daughter. The daughter lived in the downstairs studio apartment, ran right up, saw him lying unconscious on the bed and called 911. It was too late."

I ask, "Was it determined what he injected himself with?"

She grimaces, "Yes, a mixture of sodium pentothal and curare. Very lethal."

I look at her for a moment and then say, "And this little Waikiki hooker is supposed to know that." I laugh.

She also laughs. "That's their theory."

"Who are their witnesses?"

His daughter and two sons, who are the plaintiffs, the pathologist who did the autopsy and the lawyer who did the doctors will. Oh yes, they'll probably call our client as a witness. We don't have any witnesses. There's no economist since there's no economic loss."

I look at the file. "Their attorney is Brian Carter. I've never heard of him. Who's he?"

"I checked him out. He specializes in probate work and really doesn't do much, if any, trial work. He also sued to set aside the will. The claims are incompetency and that she used undue influence while he was using dope."

"This isn't probate court," I reply, "So most of that has no relevance. Why not call Carter and tell him we'll stipulate to the authenticity of the will and the pathology report. How did our client do at the deposition?"

Julie smiles. "About as well as can be expected for a twenty-one year old hooker with an IQ to match her age."

I laugh. "How come she married the guy?"

Julie also laughs. "I imagine she was mining for gold. And, it looks like she hit the mother lode. He left an estate of two million dollars not counting the house which is worth at least six hundred thousand."

"Have her come in so we can talk to her about her testimony. I'm sure we'll get a directed verdict, but we should still prepare jury instructions."

"They're all done. My secretary is finishing them now. Also, I'll do some research on the duty a wife owes under these circumstances."

I sit back and relax. "Good idea. I can't believe it. I'm actually going to have a free weekend."

A Reasonable Person

"Don't get too relaxed. The following week you have a tough one. The assault and battery at Club Satellite."

I ask, "Isn't that the one where the doorman threw the plaintiff out of the club for being loud and obnoxious?"

"That's right. David has been prepping it. Do you want to see him?"

Before I can answer, the intercom announces that the jury has reached a verdict. I tell Julie, "Tell David to walk to court with me and he can tell me about the Club Satellite case."

An hour later David and I are in Jacks, a downtown bar with a happy hour that seemingly lasts forever. We're sitting in a corner booth which is comparatively quiet for this hour.

David raises his glass and says, "Congratulations, another defense verdict."

I touch his glass with my bottle of beer. "Thank you but it was almost a slam dunk. I hear the Club Satellite case may be more difficult."

David says, "It's certainly no slam dunk. Do you remember the basic facts?"

I take a sip of beer. "As I recall, the plaintiff was escorted off the premises by the manager and one of the doormen. He's claiming they kicked him in the testicles and roughed him up pretty good including breaking his nose. Right so far?"

"Yes. He claims he was short changed, complained and was treated rather badly. The manager and doorman claim he was drunk, making a big scene and refused to leave, so they escorted him outside using hardly any force. Once outside, he again refused to leave and they took him to the security office where he was photographed and a police officer was called to escort him off the premises. However, he slammed his fist through a window and they called 911 to get him to emergency."

I ask, "What happened at emergency?"

"They x-rayed his hand, found no fractures, taped it and sent him home. No mention of any complaints about his nose."

"As I recall," I say, "When the sheriff served the owner of the club with the complaint he also served him with a notice of the taking of the depositions of the plaintiff's guests. I was at their depositions and they basically corroborated what the plaintiff says. However, neither the manager nor the doorman had been served so I don't think the depositions can be used in court. Please research it and prepare a memo."

"Okay. Also, we should take the deposition of the doctor who operated on him. He's on Kauai."

I finish my beer. "Schedule it for next Thursday or Friday. My trial on Monday can't take more than three days. Also, have everyone share the cost of bringing him to Honolulu. That would be cheaper than three of us traveling to Kauai. Are any other depositions necessary?"

"I don't think so," David replies. "We took the deposition of the plaintiff and the plaintiff's attorney took the depositions of the manager, the doorman and the security officer. Also, we deposed the emergency room doctor. I can't think of anyone else."

He looks at me, and I think about it for a moment before replying, "No, me either."

David then asks, "What about your trial for this coming Monday? Anything I can do to help?"

"Thanks, I reply, "But that one is all ready to go. As I told Julie, it should be a directed verdict."

David laughs. "And it's only Wednesday. You can take off for the rest of the week."

I nod to the waitress, pay the bill and leave a couple of dollars on the table for her. I say to David, "There's always something to do. My desk is still piled high with paperwork but I'll start on it tomorrow. I'm heading home."

Chapter 20

8:30 A.M.:

It's Friday morning and I'm on my first cup of coffee. My desk is clear thanks to my efforts of the past two days. I actually slept in this morning after working late last night. Before leaving home this morning, I kissed Kathy goodbye and told her I might play golf this afternoon. I take a sip of coffee and think that I'll make some calls and set up lunch and a golf game at the club.

As I reach for the phone Eve Lee enters the room. Eve is one of our two bookkeepers. She's of Irish descent, in her mid-fifties with dark brown hair showing traces of grey. She's hard working, smart and very competent.

As she enters she closes the door and says, "Good morning Mark," and sits in one of my client chairs. She appears to be softly crying.

I hand her a Kleenex and ask, "Eve, What's the problem?"

She sighs. "What I'm about to tell you is very confidential. You must promise me not to tell anyone."

"Of course. You know you can trust me. After all, we've known each other for almost twelve years." It's hard to believe that she's been working for me for so long.

She continues, "You know that I've been married for over thirty years?"

I smile, "Of course. Kathy and I were at your thirtieth anniversary party. It was the best Chinese food I've ever had."

She says, "Albert has been cheating on me for more than five years."

I stare at her. Albert is Chinese-American, in his early sixties. A civil engineer, he worked for the Department of Transportation for thirty-five years and retired about five years ago. "Albert! You've got to be kidding. How do you know?"

She starts to sob. "He told me. He said he sees her almost every afternoon, and now they want to be together all the time. He wants a divorce."

I move over to the chair next to her and hand her the box of Kleenex. I don't know what to say. "Eve, I'm really sorry," is all I can blurt out. I hold her hand.

After a few minutes she stops crying. "What do you think I should do?"

"Maybe he's going through some sort of mid-life crisis. Have you discussed counseling with him?"

She nods. "Yes, but he says at sixty-three he's past mid-life and refuses to go to any counseling. He's insisting on a divorce." She has completely stopped crying and sits straighter.

I walk back to my chair, sit and ask her, knowing the answer. "What do you want to do?"

She looks down, "My feeling is that if he wants a divorce so badly, then that's what he's going to get. But I want the best divorce lawyer in Honolulu to represent me."

"You know that we don't handle family matters, but I know some good lawyers who do. I can make some phone calls."

"Good, I would appreciate that. But, there is something else."

I knew it. "Go ahead."

"We own several houses. After the divorce is finalized I want to take my share and move to Las Vegas. With the proceeds I should be able to buy a nice house there."

I ask her, "Is that where your children are?"

"Yes, both of them are there and I want to be near them."

I can see her mind is made up. "I don't blame you, but we're going to miss you around here."

She looks at me and smiles. "I'll miss all of you, too. Especially you, and I'll even miss Frank. I promise that I won't leave until a good replacement is broken in."

I tell her, "I appreciate that and I know you too well to think you would do otherwise."

I get up and walk over to her. She stands and we put our arms around each other in a huge hug. She starts crying again, breaks off and starts to leave. I feel terribly sorry for her, and it's hard to feel much sympathy for her soon-to-be ex-husband. And so it would be if I ever decided to leave Kathy. She's well liked and everyone who knows us will side with her and wonder what got into me walking away from such an enviable relationship. They'll regard me as a selfish stupid bastard. I try not to think about this as I comfort Eve.

As she goes, I tell her that I'll make some phone calls. The first lawyer I call is a female ogre, tough as nails. At first she says she's too busy but I sweet talk her for a few minutes, and she agrees to see Eve. We set up an appointment, and I walk to Eve's office which she shares with Ann Kobayashi, our senior bookkeeper. I give her the information about the lawyer and appointment then go into the coffee room for a fresh cup. I return to my office and look at my watch.

9:30 A.M.:

I reach for the phone, but before I can pick it up Ellen rushes into the room shuts the door and sits. "Good morning, Mark," she says.

"Good morning Ellen," I reply. "What's happening?" Ellen is our office manager, a very attractive, but also very tough Korean woman. She married an American soldier to be admitted to the United States and on becoming a citizen divorced him. She's been seeking to marry a rich American for as long as I can remember, but so far hasn't been successful. She's worked for us for close to ten years. One of her functions is the hiring of all non-legal personnel.

"I have a little problem that I thought I should discuss with you."

I frown. Normally she doesn't bother me with details. I lean back in my chair, take a sip of coffee, and ask, "What's the problem?"

She also leans back and says, "Janice gave us notice, so I've been interviewing for a new secretary. I have an applicant who meets all the requirements. An excellent typist, good at shorthand, though that's not necessary any more, several years experience as a legal secretary with an emphasis in litigation."

I shrug. "Sounds good to me. What's the problem? If it's money I'm sure we can work it out. Why not hire her?"

"It's not money, and I don't think it's a her."

I'm puzzled. "What do you mean?"

Ellen gives me a half-hearted smile. "I think she's a man. Or, at least, was a man. She's wearing a dress with high heels but underneath she's a he."

I smile. "How do you know? Did you sneak a peek?"

She gives me a dirty look. "Of course not! But she's over six feet tall and must weigh well over two hundred pounds. Her arms are bulging with muscles. She must be a man. I don't know what to do."

I can't help but smile. "I think the first thing is to determine if she's a she or a he. Have you asked her?"

Now she smiles. "No, I thought I'd leave that up to you."

"Thanks a lot. Where is she?"

"In my office. I'll go get her."

While waiting I take a few sips of coffee. Within moments, Ellen re-enters followed by a large woman dressed in a skirt that does not quite hide her knees. Her legs are muscular and her arms are lined with veins and packed with muscle. She's definitely the most masculine woman I've ever seen. Ellen introduces her to me as Roberta. I put out my arm and she shakes hands with a viselike grip. My hand goes numb and I'm certain it'll be an hour before I'll be able to use it.

I retrieve my hand and ask, "Where did you get a grip like that? You must work out every day."

She smiles. "I do like to work out." Her voice is not high pitched, but it does have a feminine tone to it.

I tell her to be seated and resume my chair. Ellen sits on my couch. I say, "It seems like you're well qualified for the position here, but why did you leave your last job?"

She answers, "I had surgery about a year ago in Baltimore, took off for a year and ended up here in Hawaii."

I think I understand. "Was the purpose of the surgery to change your gender?"

She looks me straight in the eye. "Yes. I had been a man for thirty-six years. I was a captain in the Marine Corps, won the silver star as a helicopter pilot in Nam. But, inside, I've always felt like a woman and finally decided to do something about it."

I lean back in my chair and look at Ellen. She has her eyes averted. I say to Roberta, "If we hire you do you foresee any problems? To most people around here nothing is sacred."

She shakes her head, "Not really. I'm pretty thick skinned so I can handle their jokes."

"You would have to. What restroom would you use?"

She laughs. "The womens' of course. But I'm very discreet so I don't think that'll be a problem."

I also laugh. I note that Ellen still has her eyes averted. I say, "Why don't we try you for a sixty day probationary period. If it works out we'll put you on a permanent basis."

She stands and extends her hand, "Thank you very much, Mr. Dorsey. I'm certain it will work out fine."

"I hope so. Good luck but, if you don't mind, I'd just as soon skip shaking hands."

We both smile and they leave the room. I again look at my watch.

10:15 A.M.:

I again reach for the phone, but, like a stick of dynamite, in blasts Frank. He's carrying two cups of coffee and puts one of them on my desk. "Good morning. I haven't had a chance to talk to you and thought you'd want to hear how things went."

"Good morning and thanks," I reply as I take a sip of the hot coffee. "How was New York?"

"Great! I'll tell you the important stuff first. I saw two wonderful plays. One of them, Annie, should win a Tony. The restaurants there are still marvelous. I didn't have one bad meal."

I assume that he wasn't alone but I'm not about to ask him if he brought his girlfriend along. I'll find out when I review his bills. I still remember one trip where he actually charged a dress to our client.

I ask, "How about the unimportant news like the depositions?" I add sarcastically, "You did take them?"

He smiles. "The bad news, according to his doctors, is that he is and always will be paralyzed from the waist down. The good news is that he has a terrible case and he's a horrible witness. He lied about not seeing the water safety pamphlet that was given to him when he checked in, he lied about not seeing all of the red flags on the beach, he lied about not seeing the warning signs on the beach and in front of the life guard station, and he denied that the lifeguards told him not to go in the water."

I smile. "I think you're right. It doesn't look like much of a case." Frank says, "I spoke to his attorney, and I'm sure that if we pay his costs he'll dismiss. But, do you want to hear something funny?"

I nod and he continues, "On the return flight I was sitting next to a young businessman from Iowa. He told me that he had never seen the Pacific Ocean. I told him about the case and asked him what he thought signs should say to properly warn people of any danger in the surf. He thought for a few seconds and then said he thought there should be a big sign on the beach saying 'OCEAN!'"

We both laugh and as he leaves says, "I'll dictate full reports on the depositions this afternoon."

11:00 A.M.

As he exits, my intercom announces a call on line 3. I pick it up and it's Elaine. She wants me to come to San Francisco as her husband is giving her a hard time.

I tell her it's impossible and she goes into all of the details. "You've got to," she insists. He's being a beast."

She then tells me about the problems she's having with her children, her parents and her brother. I feel like I need a drink. I listen to her for forty-five minutes and then she abruptly says goodbye and hangs up. I sit there for a few moments wondering what that was all about.

11:45 A.M.

Laurie Oliver walks in and sits. "Good morning," she says.

Laurie is a recent graduate of UCLA Law School and has been with us for about a year. She's wearing a light blue mini skirt which shows off her magnificent legs. Her blouse is as sheer as a light haze and I also admire her breasts. She was hired to assist Frank, and though I'm certain he approved her for her looks she's very smart and has worked out well for him.

"Good morning," I reply, how can I help you?"

She nods at the file on her lap. "Frank suggested that I discuss this case with you. He says it's more in your field of expertise than his. It's a referral from General Indemnity Insurance which discussed it with Frank while you were in trial."

"What's it about?"

Laurie leans forward, "It's a coverage question. The claims supervisor is adamant that there's no coverage on this, but his manager said we should send an opinion letter to cover their ass. It arises out of an incident that occurred about a year ago in Wahiawa. The insured owns a small restaurant. He was in the kitchen when it was held up by a robber who ran out the back door. The owner picked up a baseball bat, chased the guy down an alley and slammed him in the back of his head with the bat. The robber was killed. A wrongful death suit has been filed against the owner by the family of the robber." She sits back in her chair, and seems more relaxed.

A Reasonable Person

I take a sip of my now cold coffee. "I assume that General Indemnity is claiming that the owner acted intentionally so that it's not covered. Can't you send him a letter to that effect?"

She reaches into the folder and hands me a complaint. "You should look at this. It adds a wrinkle to the situation."

I quickly read the complaint. "I see what you mean. It not only alleges that the insured committed an intentional tort but also alleges negligence on his part. How could he have been negligent? He deliberately swung the bat at the guy."

She looks at me. "True, but negligence is obviously covered by his insurance policy. The company is insisting that we write a letter confirming that there's no coverage but I find that difficult due to the allegation of negligence."

"Even though there is absolutely no basis for the allegation?"

She reads to me. "The duty to defend is greater than the obligation to pay benefits. Thus, if the allegations fall within the parameters of the insurance policy, the duty to defend arises." She adds, "That's from a recent California Supreme Court case."

I ask her, "Are there any Hawaii cases?"

"No, but I'm certain with the present make up of our Supreme Court that it would follow the California decision."

I nod my head. "I agree. In your letter, you have to cite the California case and advise them that it's our opinion that, at this time, they have a duty to defend. But, we should also advise them to bring a declaratory relief action holding as a matter of law that there's no negligence so there's no duty to defend or, in the alternative, if a judge or jury finds there's no negligence, there's no duty to pay. That's not what the company may want to hear but we've got to tell them the way it is."

She asks, "Who should defend?"

"Tell them that our firm can't defend as there would be a conflict of interest. However, we can handle the declaratory relief action. Prepare the letter for my signature. If the company instructs us to proceed, I'll have you prepare the complaint and assist me in preparing and trying the case. So far you've done an excellent job."

She smiles as she rises. "Thank you. I'll dictate the letter right away, and I look forward to working with you on this." She leaves the room.

1:00 P.M.

As Laurie leaves my office Donna Black enters. Donna started out as a messenger, was promoted to receptionist and then to file clerk. Meanwhile, she took a two year para-legal course at Kapiolani Community College and for the past three years has been working as one of our top para-legals. She says, "Good morning. May I talk to you for a moment?"

I say, "Only if you ask Marsha to bring me a turkey sandwich and a cold drink." I've had more that enough coffee already. All thoughts of lunch at the club are long gone.

She steps out of the room and a moment later returns.

I motion for her to sit and ask, "Is everything alright?"

She smiles. "Everything is fine. Did you know that I got my degree from the University?"

I look at her more closely. When she first came to work for us she was seventeen and dressed like a hippie. She'd just graduated from high school. Now she's a smartly dressed twenty-five year old. "No, I didn't. Congratulations. Why haven't you said anything? What was your major?"

She replies, "I majored in pre-law and I've been accepted to law school."

I almost feel like a proud father. I get up, walk around the desk and give her a big hug. "That's wonderful. I'm very proud of you. Which law school?"

Her eyes are tearing. "Thank you. I'm proud of myself. I've been accepted at U.C. Hastings in San Francisco. I don't start until next September and I'd like to work until then. I need to save as much as I can. My parents will help me with tuition, but it'll still be pretty tight."

"Of course and I'll tell you what. If you return to work for us during the summers as a law clerk, we'll keep you on half salary during the school years."

Now it's her turn to come over and give me a big hug. "Thank you so much. Now I'll be able to devote my full time to school."

As she leaves the room Marsha enters with my turkey sandwich and a cup of coffee. I tell her about Donna.

She smiles and says, "We're going to miss her around here. She's been a wonderful worker."

"I agree. Maybe she'll work for us after she graduates law school."

Marsha shakes her head. "I doubt it. I think she's going to want to stay on the mainland. With her background and summer clerking for us she'll be grabbed up by a good San Francisco law firm."

"You're probably right," I reply, feeling dejected. "I only hope the best for her."

"Me too," Marsha says as she gets up.

2:00 P.M.

As I finish my sandwich, Marsha brings in the mail. I slowly sift through it. More lawsuits, demand letters, medical reports, requests for status reports on pending cases, answers to interrogatories and requests for production of documents. I start dictating.

6:00 P.M.

I finish my dictation and put it all on Marsha's desk for Monday. It appears that I'm the only one left in the office. I retrieve my car from the basement garage and fight the traffic driving home.

6:30 P.M.

Parking my car, I walk into the kitchen where Kathy is cooking dinner. She looks at me and says, "You look awful. That must have been one hell of a golf game."

I manage to barely gasp. "I think I can use a drink."

CHAPTER 21

It's the following Monday morning and I have an hour before the Thomas case begins. I carry my coffee and one of Freida's bran muffins into my office and sit, savoring reflections on one of the most relaxing weekends I've had in months.

Kathy and I actually played a round of golf on Saturday afternoon followed by a quiet dinner for two at the club.

On Sunday morning it was three sets of tennis with Bob Crown, Steve Goldberg and John McDowell, three of the most competent plaintiffs' lawyers in the state. They're also good on the tennis courts and we were all sweating by the end of the third set.

After the game we relaxed with cold beers on the veranda overlooking the courts. Bob Crown is in his early forties, about my height but broader in the shoulders. A basketball starter at Georgetown, he studied law at Yale and upon graduation was offered a position with a large Honolulu law firm. That lasted for about five years at which time he and several other associates started their own firm. By now, it's considered one of the finest plaintiffs' firms in Honolulu.

I brought up the motorcycle officer case which he recently tried against Frank. An off-duty officer was hired to direct traffic in and out of a construction project. He was struck by one of the contractors' trucks and is now paralyzed from the waist down. "Congratulations, Frank said you did a great job."

Bob smiled, "Actually, we both did well. The jury verdict was midway between our demand and his offer."

We had offered one million, Bob's demand was for two. "True," I replied "But that's the first time in a long time that a jury has awarded more than Frank offered."

Bob shook his head, "I was very lucky. First, my client was a twenty-nine year old clean cut police officer of Chinese-Hawaiian descent. The majority on the jury panel were of Chinese-Hawaiian descent. Poor Frank used all of his challenges, but still half the jurors had the same background as my client. Second, we had Judge Camara."

I let out a groan. "No, not him. Frank didn't mention that to me"

"Bob grinned, "Yes, and he's the only person I know who doesn't like Frank. He may be an incompetent judge but he leans over backwards for plaintiffs. And, finally," he continued "I think your insurance carrier underestimated the value of the case. Our economist testified that our client's past and future loss of earnings, reduced to present value, amounted to $750,000 and that didn't include past and future medical bills. The case was easily worth what the jury awarded, and maybe more. Frank, as usual, did a good job. It was a difficult case for him."

Though not surprised, I'm pleased that Frank has been praised by one of the most respected attorneys in the state. With all his faults, Frank always does well in a courtroom and, once again, has justified my decision to ask him to join me as a partner.

My thoughts are interrupted by Frank entering the room carrying a cup of coffee in one hand and two of Freida's apple strudels in the other. He hands one of the strudels to me. "Here's one of Freida's famous apple strudels. She told me you had your usual bran muffin so I thought you could use something sweet." He runs on as I take a big bite, "By the way, do you think her breasts are getting even larger or am I just getting older?"

I almost choke on my strudel. "Her breasts haven't changed in the past ten years and, yes, you are getting older." I continue, "I played tennis with Bob Crown yesterday and he told me that you did an excellent job on the motorcycle officer case."

Frank smiles, "Thank you. It's nice hearing that from someone as competent as Bob. That was a tough case and Camara didn't make it any easier. Why does he dislike us so much?"

"He still thinks that all defense lawyers were out to get him. Now that he's a judge he thinks he's getting even with all of us. How was your weekend?"

Frank shakes his head, "Between finishing my move and preparing for today's trial it wasn't much of a weekend. How was yours?"

"It was good. After tennis yesterday, Kathy and I lounged by our pool relaxing and reading. Then I barbequed some steaks."

Frank laughs. "Are you still burning them?"

I also have to laugh. "I received a PhD in burning steaks. That's how we learned to grill them in Iowa."

Frank rises and walks to the door. "You certainly have earned one. One of these days I'm going to beat you into the office. Who's your judge today"?

I half jokingly say, "You'll beat me in when you start walking in your sleep. Fortunately, it's Azeka. He'll be perfect for this case.

Frank leaves. I finish my coffee and strudel, slip on my jacket, pick up the folder and leave for court.

We're in chambers watching judge Azeka as he scans the court file. Azeka is a short man, perhaps five feet six inches and appears shorter behind his huge desk. But he has a fine brain, an excellent knowledge of the law and a respect for lawyers who enter his courtroom well prepared. He has little, if any, patience for those who are not prepared.

Finally, he asks, in his usual brusque and forbidding tone, "Mr. Carter, I don't understand your theory. Please explain."

Carter is of medium height with a beer barrel stomach. For a number of years he was an associate with one of the larger Honolulu firms but is now on his own, specializing in wills and probate work. His personality is as dull as his specialty. He's wearing a jet black suit with a solid light blue tie. I think to myself that since he does probate work he probably goes to a lot of funerals.

He leans forward, almost falling off his chair, and says, "Your honor, the defendant, knowing that Dr. Thomas was about to kill himself, had a duty to do her best to prevent him from doing so. In the event she couldn't stop him then she should have immediately called 911. She did nothing and as a result of her inaction, he died."

Judge Azeka asks, "Do you have any legal authority for the proposition that a wife has such a duty?"

Carter shakes his head. "No, your honor, we couldn't find any cases on point."

The judge looks at me. "Mr. Dorsey, have you found any cases setting forth the duty of a wife in a situation such as this?"

I hand the judge a three page Memorandum of Law prepared by Julie and pass a copy to Carter. "We couldn't find any cases directly on point, but, among others, we have cited a California case in which the wife did nothing to prevent her intoxicated husband from driving. The California Supreme Court held that there was no duty owed by the wife under those circumstances. We've also cited analogous cases which stand for the same proposition. There have been no Hawaiian cases on point."

Azeka quickly scans our memorandum and then turns to Carter. "It seems to me you have a difficult case. First, you have to show that the wife knew the doctor was in the process of killing himself. Second, even if she did know, you have to show she had a legal duty to either prevent him from doing so or call for help." The judge turns to me. "Any chance of settlement?"

I shake my head. "No, your honor. I've been instructed to proceed to trial."

He asks us, "Very well, how long do you think it will take?"

Carter speaks up. "We're stipulating to the pathology report and the will. The only witnesses are the wife and his children. It shouldn't take too long."

I interject. "We're stipulating to the authenticity of the will but not to its relevancy. Also, we will object to testimony of the other children as they weren't witnesses."

Carter says, "They can testify that the defendant unduly influenced the doctor into changing his will giving her a good motive for seeing him dead."

Judge Azeka leans back and for a few moments ponders the situation. He then says in a magisterial tone, "This is the way it's going to be. I will admit the pathology report into evidence. The wife and the daughter can testify. The will and any testimony concerning undue influence is not relevant. This is not a murder trial. If the plaintiff can show me convincing authority that there was a duty owed by the wife, the sons can testify as to loss of love, affection and companionship. In the absence of any such authority, I will grant a motion by defendant for a directed verdict. I'll have the bailiff bring in the panel and we'll start jury selection in fifteen minutes."

Carter and I rise and exit through the door leading to the courtroom. I'm positive that Azeka will grant a motion for directed verdict. I think to myself how much easier my life would be if all judges were as good as this one.

At five sharp, Azeka recesses for the day and I return to our offices where I join Frank, who is interviewing Sidney Morakami in the conference room. Frank hands me Sidney's resume and I'm very impressed. Sidney is a graduate of the University of Hawaii and the University of Washington Law School. He's been working for Judge Sakumoto since graduation, a little over a year ago. Of Japanese descent, he's tall, almost six feet, but slender, weighing less than one hundred fifty pounds. He tells us that he married his high school sweetheart upon graduation from college and she helped put him through law school. What especially pleases us is that he seems willing to work long hours, makes a good impression and has local ties. The fact that he's Asian is also an asset.

Sidney leaves and we move to my office where Frank takes his favorite seat on my couch and I sit behind my desk. I ask Frank, "What do you think?"

Frank seems almost detached which is not unusual for him when it comes to matters of this kind. Normally he leaves such mundane concerns as hiring and firing up to me. He replies, "I like him but he'll be working with you so it's your decision."

"Then let's hire him," I say. "He's very presentable, he won't be leaving the state and he wants to do trial work. What more can we ask?"

Frank agrees and then asks, "Speaking of trials, how did yours go today?"

"I think it went well, "I reply. "We selected the jury, made opening statements and the wife testified. Tomorrow morning is the daughter, and then, I'm fairly certain, Azeka will grant my motion for a directed verdict."

"How was the wife? Wasn't she a prostitute?"

I laugh. "She was horrible. She can hardly speak English and has a high squeaky voice. Ventura was there for her testimony and later referred to her as Minnie Mouse. Of course, the real Minnie is much smarter. By the way, who would you have wanted on the jury?"

He smiles. "Minnie Mouse, that's rich." Then, answering my question, "I'd want single young men. I think they'd tend to be less critical of her. I wouldn't want anyone older than thirty-five. But what does it really matter if Azeka is going to give you a directed verdict."

"He probably will, but there's always a small chance that he won't. I completely agree with your opinion on jury selection. Unfortunately, the panel looked like they were all bussed in from a retirement home. There were only two under sixty and one is an assistant golf pro at Oahu Country Club."

Frank lets out a loud laugh. "I assume Azeka kicked him off. It's good that Azeka is taking it away from the jury."

I then ask, "How is Laurie working out?"

"She's great," he responds. "She has a good legal mind lurking inside a fantastic body."

He gets up and walks to the door, turns around and says, "I've got to go. I have a date. See you tomorrow," and he's gone.

I look at my calendar to see what's set for trial next Monday. Oh yes, the Club Satellite case. As David said, it's no slam dunk. I decide to look it over before going home. I pick up the phone and ask David to bring in the file. While waiting for him, I lean back and let my thoughts stray. Inevitably at such moments they attach themselves to Elaine and despite the guilt I feel, the thought of being with her again possesses me completely.

Part II |

August, 1980
The Mainland

Chapter 22

The first class section of the 727 is nearly empty, only ten seats to begin with and a mere four taken. The flight is due in Omaha at midnight. I stare out the window. No lights below, no stars above. Looking around the dark cabin, I hear no sounds except the constant droning of the jet engines pulling us closer to Omaha.

The darkness surrounding me matches my mood. I feel as dark as the sky. Glancing at my watch, I see that we'll be landing in thirty minutes. Next to me, Kathy is sleeping soundly, her head curled on her shoulder, snoring slightly, no, just a deep breathing regular and calm. At least she's undisturbed. I close my eyes and think about my deposition schedule. I'm too worn out to think about much beyond that.

My travel schedule is going as planned. I spent three days in San Francisco. Kathy arrived in time to meet me for our flight to Omaha. She must be exhausted, having been in meetings until time for her flight from Honolulu. We'll arrive at midnight, pick up a rental car and check into a hotel. The deposition starts at 9:00 A.M. tomorrow and shouldn't take more than two hours.

Kathy and I will have lunch, spend the afternoon in Omaha, then catch the 6:00 P.M. flight to Houston with depositions the next day. Off to Chicago for more depos, and then to Toronto for several days of more hotels, rental cars, restaurants and depos. What a way to make a living! At least, I think, the good part is that I'll be out of the office for a week.

The seat belt sign flashes, passengers are directed to buckle up and we start our descent into the Omaha Airport. I'm still musing upon my brief stay in San Francisco.

The red eye from Honolulu deposited me there at 5:00 AM on Saturday. I rented a car and checked into the hotel, catching a few hours of sleep before my meeting. I slept for a few hours and then went to my meeting. We broke up at noon and I returned to the hotel to meet Elaine.

On seeing her I again marveled at how attractive she looked, ageless and irresistible. I asked where she'd like to have lunch. She responded, "Lunch can wait. Let's go to your room. I have to talk to you."

Once in my room, I opened the drapes and we looked out the big picture windows to a spectacular view which even gave us a glimpse of Sausalito in the distance. It was one of those special San Francisco days, blue and beautiful with not a hint of fog or haze. I said, "You look great. All I have to do is look at you and I get turned on."

She leaned against me and I put my arms around her. She said, "I've missed you. We haven't seen each other for months."

"I've missed you, too."

"Tell me, how did your meeting go?"

"The meeting was with a client of mine, Professional Insurance Company," I answered. "They screwed up on a case and got sued for bad faith. We're trying to settle and I met with some of their people who came in from Ohio. We'll meet again on Monday. The plaintiff's attorney is coming in from Seattle and I'm sure we'll settle."

Not having the slightest idea or interest in what I was talking about, she said, "I like your suit but wouldn't you be more comfortable in shorts?"

I laughed, "Absolutely! But I don't think I'd have made a very good impression on those city slickers in shorts. If you don't mind, I'll put on a robe."

She smiled, "Good idea. Is there one there for me?"

Later, lying in bed, her head resting on my chest, she gave me the news. "I've got something important to tell you. I've left my husband and filed for divorce."

I was somewhat surprised as I never truly thought she'd do it. I didn't say anything for a full minute. Finally I asked, "When did it happen? Tell me more."

She turned on her back and lit a cigarette. "He moved out about two months ago. I didn't want to talk about it on the phone. I started divorce proceedings and our attorneys are working out a settlement. I bet you never thought I'd do it."

She would have won the bet. "What about your plan? Will it work out financially for you?" I turned toward her and stroked her hair. Dark red and fine, it felt silky-smooth to my touch.

She shook her head. "He can't quit gambling. He's addicted to it. But he'll pay all household expenses including mortgage payments, as well as support for me and the children. It won't be high living but we'll get along. We're already happier with him out of the house."

Always the lawyer, I asked, "What about the business?"

She said, "That and the house are the major areas of contention between us. But, actually, my main concern is you."

"What do you mean? Why should I concern you?"

She put out her cigarette, turned to face me and said, "I took a big step, but I want to make it clear that my breaking up has nothing directly to do with you. I would have left my husband whether you were in the picture or not." She paused for a moment and then went on. "However, you are in the picture. You know that I love you very much. I'm sure you love me. But things are different now."

I broke in, "Why?"

"Because you're married and I'm not or soon won't be. You're going to have to make a decision. Once I'm officially single, seeing you only once or twice a year won't work."

I turned on my back. "What you're saying is that I leave my wife or we don't see each other again."

She lit another cigarette. "You don't have to decide right away."

"When?" I asked.

"Not until I go to court. Several months, I guess. Meanwhile, since I have no husband at home why don't you ask me to stay the night?"

I smiled, "Of course, but what about your kids?"

"I told them I'd be staying in the city tonight, and I have an overnight bag in my car. Always prepared." Then she asked rhetorically, "Was I being presumptuous?"

Instead of answering her question, I looked at my watch. "Almost time for dinner. Where do you want to eat?"

She slipped off her robe and rolled over on top of me. "First things first."

Jarring me from my reverie is the jerking of the plane as the wheels descend and I watch the 'No Smoking' sign light up. A droning voice orders all seats placed back in their upright positions. I obediently put my seat into the required position and look out the window as the ground rushes to greet us.

I let out my breath as the 727 floats down gently, like the cardinals in my backyard, their red crowned heads glowing in the reflection of the pool. I look at Kathy, her eyes now open, and say, "Great landing. Must be a flight attendant doing the work."

She laughs. "No, just the co-pilot. By the way where are we staying?"

"A Hilton by the airport. We really don't have much of a choice in Omaha."

"I'm glad it's by the airport. I'm exhausted."

The plane taxies to the ramp area, the seat belt sign goes off and the passengers behind us are loudly lunging at the overhead racks for their carry-on luggage. Kathy and I pick up our items and patiently wait for the door to open. While waiting, she admires a pendant the flight attendant is wearing and tells her. The attendant, an older woman, is gratified and thanks her for the compliment. Kathy has a knack of making people, both men and women, feel good about themselves. They readily sense that she is sincere and are attracted by her natural wholesome charm.

At midnight, the routine of reclaiming our luggage, getting a rental car and checking into the hotel goes quickly and smoothly. By the time I brush my teeth and set my travel alarm she's fallen asleep. The last sound I remember hearing is a jet taking off from the nearby airport, probably heading back to San Francisco. I close my eyes and try not to think of Elaine.

CHAPTER 23

Early the following morning, over a light breakfast, Kathy asks me about today's case.

Between bites of a toasted English muffin, I tell her, "The Morrisons, two tourists from Omaha, were staying at the Queen Kaiulani Hotel. They were rudely awakened by three Asian men about 1:00 A.M. The intruders had been given the wrong room key by a very busy room clerk who stated that she was trying to check in a group of kids wearing University of Texas sweatshirts. She claimed that they may have had too much to drink on their flight. But, according to the hotel staff, they were just a group of students who were behaving themselves."

Kathy smiles. "Being woken up in the early morning by three strangers is not my idea of fun."

"True," I agree, "But Morrison completely over- reacted. He called the desk clerk demanding that the police be called. The clerk sent up a security officer who immediately saw what happened and took the men back to the lobby. Morrison threw on some clothes and followed them down with his poor wife trailing behind. Once in the lobby, he started screaming at the clerk and security officer that there was a 'conspiracy' going on and kept insisting they call the police."

"Conspiracy?" Kathy asks. What kind of conspiracy?"

"I don't know. Maybe he was thinking of Watergate," I say jokingly and continue. "The staff tried to calm him down and explain but he refused to listen. Then he said he thought he was having a heart attack and insisted they call an ambulance to take him to emergency. Instead they called a cab."

"Did he have a heart attack?" she asks.

"Hell no. At emergency they did some tests, gave him a sedative and sent him back to the hotel. Now he's suing the hotel."

Kathy looks at me with surprise. "You mean the case is about a desk clerk handing out the wrong key? That's it? What's he suing for?"

"Negligent infliction of serious mental distress. When he returned home, his family doctor referred him to a psychiatrist but he only went two or three times. As far as we know, there's been no further treatment."

Kathy shakes her head. "I can't believe they'd send you here for this."

"Ventura thought that since I'd be in the area, I might as well take his deposition. It shouldn't take too long and maybe I can settle it. Are you still planning on visiting your aunt?"

"She smiles. "Yes, I'm looking forward to it. It's been years since I've seen her."

"Good, I'll call you when I'm done, it should be before noon. Maybe your aunt can join us for lunch."

"That would be great," she replies. "Shouldn't we be going? It's almost nine, and we have to find the lawyer's office."

It's so typical. She's always interested in my cases, and now she's the one watching the clock to make sure I'm at my appointment on time. A man couldn't have a more supportive wife.

We have no problem finding the office in West Omaha. It's in a small two story dismal brown Spanish style building that looks like it belongs in southern California rather than Omaha. As I watch her drive away, I think what a wonderful, unselfish, good hearted woman she is. The exact opposite of Elaine, who is self-centered, selfish and crafty. Why am I so obsessed with her? The heart has reasons, so they say, but when I compare these two women in my life I have to laugh at my folly for letting Elaine captivate me.

Entering the building, I see a small sign indicating that Goldman shares offices with several other lawyers on the second floor. I decide to walk up, not chancing the cubbyhole of an elevator which appears incapable of rising to the second floor. I enter the offices and hear the all familiar law office sounds of clicking typewriters and the murmuring of female voices.

The receptionist is a wholesome looking, attractive young woman who, even though half-hidden behind a counter, is obviously well endowed. She stops her typing, looks up and asks, "May I help you?"

"Yes," I respond as I hand her my card. "I'm here for a deposition with Mr. Goldman."

She sighs, "Oh, you're from Hawaii. I've never been there." Her look implies that she'd love to climb into my briefcase and return with me. Maybe twenty years ago.

We're interrupted by a tall, dark haired man, obviously Elliott Goldman. He's wearing an expensive looking pastel shirt with a thin pin striped tie. No jacket. We introduce ourselves and he shakes my hand with a grip that could squeeze blood from a top sirloin.

I take a closer look, noting that he's not only tall but heavily built. In his mid-forties, Goldman has a strong looking face with good features, and he emits an aura of charm and intelligence, a likeable person who can readily inspire confidence in his clients. I sum him up as a good lawyer but without the killer instinct it sometimes takes to be a good trial lawyer. As Frank, in his inimitable manner would put it, "A nice guy, but he ain't no Piranha."

"We have a few minutes, would you like a cup of coffee?" He asks.

I nod my head and follow him into his office. It's a warm and friendly room with thick beige carpeting and a huge desk which barely leaves room for two comfortable looking client chairs.

I'm drawn to a large picture window overlooking a wide busy street, beyond which extends an endless expanse of flat brown earth. I can't imagine living here after being so long in the verdant and blue brilliance of Hawaii. Goldman stands next to me and says, "I bet this doesn't remind you of home."

I smile. "Actually, I'm originally from Iowa, which is similar, but this is nothing like Hawaii. On a clear day you can probably see Chicago. Have you lived here all your life?"

"Of course," he laughs, "Do you think anyone would move here on purpose?"

I also laugh. "No, I guess not, but I don't remember Iowa being so flat. Is all of Nebraska like this?"

"All that I've seen, but I make it a point of trying not to travel much in Nebraska."

I sit, and Goldman says, without a pause between sentences, "How was your trip? I've never been to Hawaii. I'd love to go there."

He starts to continue, but I break in, "Hold on a moment. First, tell me about Omaha. I want to take my wife shopping after lunch. Do you have any recommendations?"

He smiles, "I'd suggest 'New Town', but I don't think you'll have much chance for shopping. Are you flying out tonight?"

"Yes", I reply, "Our flight leaves at six. These depositions shouldn't take too long, should they?" I don't want to spend all day on such an insignificant case, but I keep that thought to myself. Many lawyers take it as a personal affront if you belittle their case.

Elliott looks thoughtful, "If I were you, I'd reach the same conclusion, but you may be surprised."

I mentally review the answers to interrogatories which had been filed months earlier. Morrison's family doctor checked him out for chest pains, found nothing wrong, referred him to a psychiatrist whose diagnosis was 'mid-life depressive syndrome'. Total medical bills were less than $500.00, loss of earnings were $6,000.00.

Goldman rises and says, "My clients are in the conference room, shall we go?"

I also rise and follow him out the door. It's difficult to believe that such an innocuous incident could have a long term effect. This seems to be confirmed by the medical records. I have no idea what Goldman means, but I'm sure I'll find out. "Okay," I say, "Let's go."

We enter a modest conference room. The Morrisons are seated on one side of a small table. Sitting at the end is the court reporter, inserting paper into her machine. Goldman makes the introductions. Mrs. Morrison is middle aged, a little over five feet, with a thin body and thin face. She looks tired, not physically tired but more like she's just tired of it all. I know the feeling. Mr. Morrison is in his early fifties, but looks ten years older, very tall, but twenty-five pounds overweight, soft looking with big sad pale blue eyes. He might have been considered good looking when young, but those days are long gone.

The court reporter hands me a business card reading, 'Naomi Gerber, Certified Shorthand Reporter." She's in her mid twenties, also well developed. I think that most Nebraskan girls must be well fed. I hand her one of my cards and she says, "You really are from Hawaii. How's the job market for court reporters there?"

It seems that every mainland reporter under thirty wants to move to Hawaii, but I reply, "We have plenty of litigation, so I'm sure you wouldn't have a problem."

Naomi sighs. "I guess it's just a daydream." With that, she swears in the witnesses and the depositions begin.

CHAPTER 24

I pride myself on having the ability to ask incisive questions, getting to the point quickly without wasting an unnecessary amount of time. But Morrison would test the patience of Mahatma Ghandi. Pulling teeth is easier than getting an answer out of him. He has difficulty remembering even the most rudimentary facts concerning his life, his business, his children or his trip to Hawaii.

With the assistance of his wife, Morrison testifies that he quit high school in 1944 to join the marines. After his discharge, he worked in the service department of a local oil company, repairing gasoline pumps and other assorted equipment. Within a few years, he was promoted to manager. Ten years later, he bought the division and now it's being operated by his two sons.

My next line of questioning is about the incident at the hotel. In a flat, unemotional tone, he tries to tell me about the event. He testifies that upon being awakened, he first thought his wife had been killed and the hotel was trying to cover it up. He relates how he argued with all of the hotel employees until he thought he was having a heart attack. At this point, Morrison is virtually hysterical and actually starts crying. I call for a break, Goldman agrees. We've been at it for two hours. I think to myself, once again, that to become intentionally involved in this type of legal practice must be an indication of some form of mental aberration. I plan on having a long talk with Rachel about her future legal career.

Elliott and I return to his office and I settle into one of his comfortable leather chairs. Elliott's secretary brings us coffee. For a few moments we sip our coffee without speaking. Finally, Elliott says, "What do you think?"

I gaze out the window at the flat brown landscape, asking myself, 'How do I tell him that he's got a nutcase for a client?' Instead I take another sip of coffee, laugh and say, "You're probably right. I'll be lucky to make my 6:00 P.M. flight."

"Actually, you're moving along faster than I thought you would. You've gotten more out of him in the past two hours than we have in the past two years." He again asks, "What do you think?"

I answer, slowly, "Obviously he has some problems, but I find it difficult to believe they all began with the incident at the hotel."

Elliott laughs. "He certainly had problems before the incident, but he seemed to be getting along in his business and personal life. Now, as you can see, he's all screwed up. A typical egg shell plaintiff, or isn't that the law in Hawaii?"

I think about it for a moment. What he means is that a defendant must take a plaintiff as he finds him. If a person has a weak back which is injured in an accident, the defendant would be responsible for all of his present back problems. This is true, even though a person with a normal back wouldn't have been as seriously injured. As one professor put it, 'if you're going to do an injury, do it to a rock, not an egg. Otherwise, you'll end up paying for a scrambled egg.' Under this theory, the hotel would be responsible for all of his present mental problems. This obviously casts a different light on the case.

I look at Goldman with new respect. "Yes, that is the law in Hawaii." With that, we return to the conference room.

Questioning Morrison further about the night at the hotel, he testifies that though he thought his wife had been killed, he never mentioned it to any of the hotel employees. He doesn't remember her being in the cab which took them to emergency, her being at emergency with him, or returning to the hotel with her.

He further testifies that on the following day, the assistant manager apologized and explained what happened but Morrison didn't believe him and still feels that the hotel was trying to cover up the incident.

Next, I question Morrison about the rest of his vacation. After several days on Oahu, he and his wife travelled to Maui for four days of sightseeing, swimming and generally having a good time. Though he now claims he had headaches and dizzy spells, he saw no doctors nor did he take any type of medication other than his regular heart pills.

The more questions I ask, the more bizarre he acts. He's constantly asking his wife for assistance in answering the most basic of questions.

A Reasonable Person

Another hour has gone by and it's now noon. I turn to Elliott and say, "How about a lunch break?"

"Great," he replies. "Let me talk to my clients for a moment and I'll be right with you."

Walking out to the reception area, the buxom receptionist tells me that my wife called and left a message saying since I was still in the deposition she would have lunch with her aunt. I sit in the reception area waiting for Elliott.

Within minutes, he and the Morrisons enter the area. Elliott tells them. "Be back in an hour." They nod and walk out.

Elliott then turns to me and says, "How would you like the best hamburger in Omaha?"

"I'm more than ready," I reply, "But it's my treat."

As we walk out, he says, "You're going to love it."

Chapter 25

Walking to the restaurant, we feel the suffocating Nebraska summer heat closing in on us. There isn't a cloud in the sky, but the color isn't the radiant, splendid blue of Hawaii, but rather an almost smoggy, gingery-amber type of blue that not only looks but also feels oppressive. The cold atmosphere of the air-conditioned restaurant is a welcome relief.

Elliott suggests the 'All-Nebraska Special Cheeseburgers' with everything on them including grilled onions. I concur, thinking how fortunate I am to have a cast iron stomach. We also order iced tea.

The tea comes in massive frosted glasses and Elliott guzzles his down in large gulps, catches the eye of the waitress and points to his glass for a refill. He asks me, "How long have you lived in Hawaii?"

"Almost twenty years," I respond.

"Why did you move? Didn't you like Iowa?"

Usually when asked this, I typically answer by quipping about the weather or traffic and extol the wonderful weather in Hawaii. But, looking at Elliott, I see real interest in his eyes and not just a desire to make superficial conversation. I see in Elliott the classic small town family doctor or lawyer, one whom you can trust with your deepest secrets, your money or your wife. Well, I think, maybe not your wife.

I don't normally divulge my past to many people but tell Elliott, "I left Iowa in 1955 to attend the University of Arizona Law School and never looked back. In 1961, I was working for a Phoenix law firm when my wife died leaving me with two young daughters. I felt I needed a change and interviewed for a job as claims counsel with an insurance company in

Hawaii. When they offered me the position, I took it. It turned out to be a good decision, for me and my daughters."

I don't share the memories of that painful time that still cause me to have some bitter feelings. I was considered one of the favorites in the office and stood an excellent chance of making partner within a few years. After my first year I was assigned to the top litigator in the firm, assisting in the trials of major cases. By my third year I was trying cases on my own. Then Lisa died of an overdose.

Omitting this tragic event, I continue, "After taking the job and moving to Hawaii, I passed the Hawaiian bar exam. I worked for the company for over two years, decided I liked Hawaii and opened my own office specializing in insurance defense. Now, here I am in Omaha taking depositions."

At this point the waitress returns with two of the largest hamburgers I've ever seen. Each looks like a pound of meat placed in fresh home baked buns, covered with dripping cheese and smothered in grilled onions. They certainly look tastier than the turkey sandwiches I've become accustomed to. I bite into mine and agree with Elliott that this is by far the best burger I've ever eaten.

As we devour our burgers in silence, I recall my turbulent marriage with Lisa which ended with her death. When I met her, she was working as a nurse at the University's medical clinic. I was playing a pickup basketball game with some other law students when one of them suffered a sprained ankle. I took him to the clinic, met Lisa and there was an immediate mutual attraction. Fragile but vivacious, no one guessed she was addicted to every kind of pill she could get her hands on, from valium to percodan. As I started dating her I learned of her troubled background. She was a Polish Jew born in the Warsaw Ghetto before the start of World War II. But she was more fortunate than most. An American aunt got her out of Poland and into the United States just before the start of the war. She never saw or heard from her parents again. Presumably, they were both killed in one of the camps.

We were married as soon as I finished my second year of law school. She continued to work at the clinic until I passed the bar exam. Her drug problems became worse, but neither hospitalizations nor psychiatric treatment helped. She was always a moody person but her bad moods got darker and longer until one morning she was found in her car, dead of an overdose. Guilt, remorse and the burden of taking care of two young girls overwhelmed me. When the Hawaiian opportunity presented itself I grabbed it.

Elliott asks, "Do you enjoy practicing law in Hawaii?"

"From what I've seen," I respond, "The practice of law is about the same no matter where you live. But in many respects, it's more convenient in Honolulu than in most big cities. I only live a few miles from my office, so driving to work is easy. All of the law offices as well as the courthouse are within a radius of a few blocks. Once you park your car you seldom need it again during the day."

"Also," I add, "It's not a large legal community, so everyone gets along fairly well. It's not the type of place where lawyers harass each other unless there's a good reason. But tell me, what about you? Do you like Omaha?"

Elliott grimaces, "There's not a hell of a lot to like. The weather is horrible, hot as hell in the summer and you freeze your ass off in the winter. And growing up as one of the few Jewish boys in the Omaha school system wasn't exactly what you would call fun. But my family and my wife's family are all here and we have some good friends so I guess it's what you'd call home. Also, it's not a bad place to practice law. Most of the attorneys get along, the judges are excellent and the traffic isn't too bad."

"Also," I say, "I imagine the cost of living here isn't too high. It's appalling in Hawaii."

Elliott laughs, "Yes. That's a decided plus in our favor but I think I'd still live there if I had a choice"

I finish the last of my hamburger and say, as I pick up the bill, "The weather alone makes it worthwhile. But we better head back." I then add, tongue in cheek, "I can hardly wait to hear the rest of your client's story."

When we re-enter the conference room the Morrisons and the court reporter are waiting for us. The Morrisons continue to look as stiff and puritanical as before, obviously apprehensive as they wait for the ordeal to continue. Lois is reading a fashion magazine, probably day-dreaming of working anywhere but Omaha, but otherwise looking as disinterested in the proceedings as all court reporters look no matter where they work.

Quickly scanning my notes, I glance at Morrison and continue my questioning, concentrating on the effect the incident had on his business and personal life. He claims that both were absolutely ruined after his experience at the hotel. He testifies that prior to the incident he ran a very successful business with the assistance of his sons, but after returning to Hawaii it took him two months before he could return to work. Even then he was not mentally capable of running the business and slowly turned it over to his wife and sons.

He further testifies that his personal and social life have been destroyed and he now spends most of his days watching TV.

I look at Elliott, "I think I'm through for now, but I would like to take Mrs. Morrison's deposition and if this matter does proceed to trial reserve the right to re-depose Mr. Morrison in Honolulu prior to trial."

Elliott agrees and I look at my watch. It's almost 3:00 P.M., and the deposition I thought would take no more than one hour has taken almost five hours and is still not complete. However, I'm certain Mrs. Morrison will not take long. I'm still hoping to catch my 6:00 P.M. flight to Houston.

CHAPTER 26

As Mrs. Morrison is sworn in, I take a good look at her and am immediately reminded of my grandmother. My maternal grandparents had come to the United States from England shortly before the turn of the century, lingering long enough in Boston to have two children and then slowly moving west to finally settle in Iowa.

Their cross-country trek could be traced through the birthplaces of their four younger children: Ohio, Indiana and Missouri. I don't remember my grandfather, but my grandmother was a stern taskmaster who almost single-handedly raised and supported her six children.

When I was a child I felt that her collection of plates, cups and saucers was absolutely fascinating. Her children brought them to her from their visits around the country. Plates with dolphins from Miami, geysers from Yellowstone, mountains from Yosemite, lakes from Michigan, waterfalls from Niagara, scenes from every resort area in the Western Hemisphere. I have to laugh every time I think of the myriad items of memorabilia on my grandmother's shelves. Mrs. Morrison looks like the same breed. A stern taskmaster who probably collects plates.

I'm right about one thing. It takes less than an hour to question Mrs. Morrison. She's intelligent, quick and responsive to my questions answering them in an honest and forthright manner. Her testimony basically corroborates that of her husband insofar as the business, his heart attack and the state of her husband's activities before their trip to Hawaii. She says he's an expert in the repair and servicing of pumps and meters used in the petroleum industry. He ran the business by himself until his sons graduated high school at which time they joined him.

She testifies that after a relatively short period following his heart attack he resumed his prior level of activity. She further testifies that before the Hawaiian incident he had no memory problems and never had occasion to see a psychiatrist.

I ask, "You're saying before this trip to Hawaii you felt that he had no mental problems?

Mrs. Morrison: "He was a whole man and a good leader and a good father and the boss of all of us. The pillar of our family, I tell you."

Me: "And the change occurred following this one night?"

Mrs. Morrison: "That's right.

"Me: "But he did go back to work after returning from Hawaii?"

Mrs. Morrison: "Yes, he tried. He finished the year and though we wanted him to stay home he wouldn't give it up. He wanted to sit in the president's seat and he made a lot of bad decisions. But he was the head of the company, he was the boss and we just pacified him for at least a year. We did things behind his back that were for the best of the company because my sons and I were right in there with him. But the company started operating at a loss so we had to make changes and Chuck wasn't up to any change."

Me: "Is he working at all now?"

Mrs. Morrison: "No. He's on disability."

Me: "Is that because of his heart condition?"

Mrs Morrison: "Yes, and his bad decisions. But even if his mental condition improved he couldn't go back to work because of his heart problem."

Questioning her about the incident at the hotel, she basically confirms what her husband said. Me: "Have you determined that there was no forcible break-in?"

Mrs. Morrison: "Yes. They definitely used a key. It was too quiet, I would have known if there had been a break-in."

Me: "Did you see a chain on the inside of the door?"

Mrs. Morrison: "That's the thing we thought about afterwards. We must have expected each other to put it on. Evidently, neither one of us put it on. I did put it on the next night."

I again change the subject and ask: "How does your husband pass the time now? What does he do?"

Mrs. Morrison: "He doesn't pass the time. He just sits around on the front porch, or he watches TV, the boob tube we call it. He goes to the spa. We do let him drive the car to the spa because Dr. Ball said it would be good for him to go there.

"Me: "Do you have any kind of social life at all?"

Mrs. Morrison: "None. We never see our friends anymore. They call him the kook."

Me: "Was there anything at all, any indication whatsoever in the year or two before the incident that made you feel that he was deteriorating or mentally slipping?"

Mrs. Morrison: "Absolutely not."

Me: "I only have one more question. What I'm wondering is if there is anything you know of that may have happened in his past that would make you feel this one incident could have such a drastic effect on him?"

Mrs. Morrison: "The only thing that enters my mind is that towards the end of the war he was taken prisoner by the Japanese. He was held in a prisoner of war camp in China for almost a year. He's never really talked about it but apparently he had some very frightening experiences. He did tell me that once in a while the guards would wake them and take one of their fellow prisoners. They'd never see him again. I can't think of anything else.

With that I conclude the deposition. Elliott walks the Morrisons' out as I put my file and notepad in my briefcase. Naomi packs her machine away telling me I'll get my copy within a few weeks. As she's walking out she says, "He's really something else, isn't he?"

I reply, "He sure is. But what do you think?" At that point I'd have asked the janitor for his opinion.

"I think you may have a tough case." She then adds as she leaves the room, "Good luck." When a court reporter feels it's necessary to wish me luck I know I'm in trouble.

Elliott reappears at the door, saying, "I just met your wife. She's lovely. She said you are all packed up and ready to go, so how about a quick drink before you leave for the airport?"

A few minutes later we're in the cocktail lounge of a nearby steakhouse. Elliott and I order beers. Both of us look like we've been drained dry. Kathy asks for a vodka martini on the rocks, no extra olives. I finally say, "It's been a long day."

Kathy looks at me inquisitively, "I thought you said the deposition wouldn't take long. You've been at it all day."

I glance at Elliott and smile, "It was a little more complicated than I thought it would be. I'll tell you about it later."

A Reasonable Person

Elliott asks Kathy, "What have you been doing all day? I wouldn't think there would be much for you to do here."

Kathy's face lights up and she looks animated: "I've been having a ball. I don't know if Mark told you, but my aunt lives here. We visited shops and had lunch. This is the first chance I've had to spend some time in a mainland city for almost a year. We went to a number of shops and met some wonderful people. I'm really looking forward to the rest of our trip."

Elliott looks at her, admiring her natural charm and good looks, "Where are you going from here?"

I reply, "I have depositions tomorrow in Houston, then two days in Chicago and several days next week in Toronto."Elliott frowns, "Sounds like a horrible schedule. Do you do this often?"

"The problem is we have so many cases involving mainland visitors we don't have much choice. Normally I let associates handle these trips, but there was one matter I had to personally handle in San Francisco and I thought this would be a good chance for Kathy and me to get away for a few days." Did I just imagine it, or did Kathy give me a strange look?

As we sip our drinks, Elliott and Kathy talk some more about her day and the items of interest to her in Omaha. He tells her he's sorry we aren't staying overnight. "I know the best steak house in the Midwest and would love to take you there." He tells us.

Kathy and I are beginning to like him immensely. It's almost impossible not to like him. I wonder to myself if I should discuss settlement but decide it's premature to try to place a value on the case at this time. Instead I say, "We'll take a raincheck, we may see you back here. By the way, who are those Topeka doctors your clients were talking about?"

Elliott answers, "He's been tested and may be treated at The Menniger Clinic in Topeka. I'll send you the names of the doctors."

Kathy looks at her watch and says, "We'd better get going. We have less than an hour to catch our flight."

By the time we get to the airport, return the rental car, check our luggage and find the proper gate our flight is ready to depart. We enter the plane just as the doors are closing. We're on our way to Houston.

Chapter 27

Entering the dining room of the Houston Galleria Hotel, I look at my watch. It's 9:30 P.M. and, once again, everything has gone as scheduled. Despite the lengthy depositions and a bumpy flight I'm in a pleasant mood and ready for a drink and a good meal.

The first class section of the flight from Omaha to Houston was somewhat more crowded than the one from L.A. Mainly young business and professional men in their charcoal suits and striped ties. Once we were seated, Kathy said she was going to take a short nap. She closed her eyes and within moments dropped off, slumbering through most of the flight.

The dining room of the Houston Galleria is elegant. Plush booths surrounded by deep red and black lined velvet wallpaper. Kathy and I are impressed. I'm wearing my best, but now dated, blue suit with a slim striped tie and Kathy has on one of her more expensive dresses, also a navy blue, with a simple pearl necklace.

The maitre'd doesn't appear to be as impressed with us as we are with the restaurant. Though he's only in his late thirties, he acts like a pompous old man as he leads us to a small table in the middle of the room. I look around, see four empty booths, and ask, "Don't you have a quiet booth for us?"

He answers as though we're from outer space, "All of our booths are reserved."

Kathy notices a vase of antheriums sitting on a small table in the corner and says to the man, "Like those antheriums, we're also from Hawaii and also need our privacy."

A Reasonable Person

Suddenly there's an entire change in his expression. He starts laughing and says, "So am I. My name is George Hughes. I was the headwaiter at the Kahala Hotel for six years. Do you live on Oahu?"

I answer, "Right down the street from the hotel by Diamond Head."

"I lived on Aukai Street, probably only a few blocks from you. I think I can give you a nice private booth over here. "As he leads us to a beautifully secluded corner booth, he adds, "What would you like to drink? The drinks are on the house."

Kathy and I ask for vodka martinis on the rocks and he relays the order to a waiter as he sits with us. Upon hearing that I'm an attorney he alludes to several Honolulu lawyers whom we both know. We talk about Honolulu for a few minutes and then he offers his hand saying, "I'm sorry I was a bit rude, but it's been a tough night. Have a great meal. I'd suggest you stay away from the fish. The veal chop and steaks are excellent. If you're in town tomorrow night try the Golden Pheasant. It's only a short cab ride and has the best food in town."

I shake hands with him and joke, "At the price of your drinks we figure we'll just sit here drinking and forget about eating."

As he walks away Kathy remarks in imitation pidgin English, "Lucky we be from Hawaii."

I smile, "Yeah, it's usually good for a nice booth and free drinks."

As we enjoy our drinks, Kathy says, "Tell me about the depositions today. How did they go?"

I grimace, "It was dreadful. According to his wife all he does is sit on the front porch staring at the horizon."

Kathy looks astonished, "You mean just from the hotel incident?"

"That's what they say. It seems hard to believe. I agree he was scared but it's difficult to accept that the incident has had such a profound impact on his life. He maintains he can hardly remember anything, the ages of his children, his doctors' names, basic facts we all take for granted. He further claims he had to retire from a good business because he was driving away customers and couldn't do the work anymore. His sons and wife have had to take over the company. His wife describes him as being almost childlike in his behavior."

The waiter interrupts us. We each order top sirloins, salads with house dressing and another drink. I then continue, "I certainly believe the hotel was negligent but I also believe he overreacted to the situation. He wouldn't believe it was just a mistake on the part of the clerk. He continued to insist burglars had broken into his room even though there was no sign of a forcible entry and even though he took the key away from one of the intruders."

"Sounds like he must have been a little off to begin with. But why is the hotel negligent?"

"First of all, the standard for determining negligence is the reasonable person test. The question is whether a reasonable person, in this case a reasonable hotel clerk, would under the same circumstances give out the wrong key. In my opinion a reasonable clerk should, even though very busy, still double check to make certain she's giving out the proper key.

"Second, I agree with you, that in all probability, Morrison was a little off to begin with. I'm sure his elevator didn't go all the way to the top floor before the incident at the hotel. But, as Elliott so astutely pointed out, he seemed to be managing his life, both in business and socially, before the incident and if what happened at the hotel caused him to break down, even though he was prone to do so anyway, the hotel could be found liable for all of his existing problems."

The waiter places two fresh drinks in front of us and tells us our salads are on the way. I feel more relaxed than I have in a long time. The drink tastes great and I'm looking forward to a good steak. I then continue, "We do have him on a few points, though. There may be some comparative negligence and I don't think a jury is going to like him too much."

"Why is that?"

"There's a clear sign on the inside of the door warning guests to put on the chain. They didn't do so, and he tried to justify this by saying he didn't have to do it at home. Also, he kept saying he thought his wife had been raped and killed. Yet he never seemed to have the slightest interest in her welfare. He never checked to see how she was, never told the security officer or the police about her, never asked for a doctor or an ambulance for her. All he seemed to care about was himself. I don't think a jury is going to think too highly of him."

The waiter brings our salads, and as Kathy takes a bite she says, "I agree. But what about the problems with his business?"

I'm constantly surprised by her insight. "That's a difficult issue. If a jury believes he couldn't continue his business because of the occurrence, then the damages for that alone could be substantial." I continue, "The salad is great, isn't it?"

"Yes, it is. What are you going to do next?"

I wisecrack, "Eat my steak." Then seriously, "I'm going to subpoena all of his updated medical records including the psychiatric records from

Menniger Clinic. I'll retain a psychiatrist in Honolulu to review all of the records and give us his opinion plus any other help he can offer. We'll file special interrogatories concerning his business to get the names of all of his customers and obtain the company's financial records for the past five years. If necessary, we'll have them completely audited so we'll know exactly what the state of his business was before and after the incident. We'll then hire a private investigator to check out his background and to find out if he quit the business because of the hotel incident or for some other reason. After that I'll take whatever depositions may be necessary, including his sons and the Kansas psychiatrists."

"Wow!" she says, "You really are thorough."

Two superb looking steaks are put before us. "You have to be in this business," I say, "Otherwise you lose, and I don't like losing."

For a few minutes we quietly enjoy our steaks. Kathy then asks, "What's your case about tomorrow?"

"It's another hotel case but this one is a little different. A fifteen-year-old boy went through a lanai door at the Kona Beach Hotel on the Big Island. His arm was badly cut up. As a result he has some serious scars and some loss of use of his arm. He claims he was on his High School baseball team and this has ruined his chances for a major league baseball career."

Kathy looks like she's going to break into tears. "Poor kid. That sounds serious. But didn't you just have a case like that?"

"The one you're thinking of was a moped accident where a high school football star had a seriously injured foot. He claimed his chances for a professional football career were ruined because of the accident."

My thoughts go back to that case. The young man had been an all state linebacker at Lahainaluna High School on Maui. He had barely graduated when a van made a quick left turn in front of his moped. Though he hadn't received any college scholarships he still claimed his dream of being an NFL star was ruined because of the accident. I retained the head of a large NFL recruiting company to testify as an expert witness. He testified that the boy's chances of being selected by an NFL team were absolutely zero and gave a multitude of reasons including the boy's size, speed and a number of other factors for his opinion. The jury gave the boy an award, but it was for substantially less than his lawyer had asked for and even somewhat less than the insurance carrier had offered before trial.

"But you're right," I say, "This could be a serious case. I'll take his and his parents' depositions in the morning. We have a small conference room reserved here at the hotel.

Kathy asks, "If the boy went through the lanai door how was the hotel at fault?"

"Apparently his lawyers have two theories. First, there should have been some type of warning on the sliding glass door such as decals or signs. Second there was a violation of the state building code which requires shatter proof glass in all doors."

We went back to our steaks for a moment and then Kathy asks, "How are you going to get around those theories. They sound pretty good to me."

I finish my steak thinking how nice it would be if there were beef like this in Honolulu. "Actually, I think we've got them on both points. First, there were decals on the glass door. As soon as the accident was reported the manager locked the room and called the hotel's insurance company. The company immediately hired a professional photographer to take pictures of the scene and close ups of the glass door. The pictures clearly show at least four or five decals on the door. I don't know how their lawyer thinks he's going to get around that type of evidence.

Second, at the time the hotel was built the state building code didn't require shatter proof glass. That law didn't go into effect until several years after the hotel was built. If new glass is installed it has to be shatter proof but the original doors were built according to code. So we should win on that theory also."

Kathy responds, "It sounds like you have this one under control."

"I hope so but there may be a problem area. Again, the test is what a reasonable person would or would not have done under the same or similar circumstances. In this case, even though the code regarding shatter proof glass didn't go into effect until several years after the construction of the hotel there's still a question as to whether a reasonable hotel developer should have installed shatter proof glass regardless of the code. Even though Hawaii hadn't yet required safety glass, a number of other states did. After all, it's a large resort type hotel, the developers knew that children would be there and for a few extra dollars could have made the premises substantially safer."

By now we've both finished our meal and George returns to our table asking if we'd like an after dinner drink. We both refuse, I sign the bill and we return to our room. I hope to myself that the other attorney on this case, Bill Peters of Hilo, isn't too clever.

CHAPTER 28

The following morning I take the elevator to the second floor conference room. Entering I see the court reporter has set up her machine. We introduce ourselves and exchange cards. Her name is Jan Green. After ordering coffee and sweet rolls from room service, I sit to wait for the Williams's and their attorney and for the inevitable question from the reporter.

Jan doesn't disappoint me. She immediately asks, "How is the job situation for court reporters in Honolulu?"

I give my standard reply, one I can now give in my sleep. "Not bad. There's a lot of litigation there and the reporters do very well." Mercifully, before I can continue, the door opens and four people enter the room.

Leading the way is a seventeen year old boy, blond and somewhat tanned, not too tall, well under six feet and slender, weighing no more than 135 pounds. Clean cut, pleasant looking, the all-American boy type, assuming there's such a thing in today's world as an all-American boy. Following are his parents. Neither of them appears to be over thirty. Mr. Williams is wearing a pair of gray slacks, a navy blue blazer and powder blue tie. Mrs. Williams looks absolutely outstanding in a cotton summer dress, its color matching her husband's tie. For a moment, I wonder if these are really the Williams or whether their attorney has hired three actors in order to impress me.

Following them into the room is their attorney. My secretary told me that Bill Peters had made arrangements for the referring lawyer from Houston to attend the depositions. This is my first case against Peters. We first met at the depositions of the hotel people and I found him to be a personable and seemingly competent young attorney. I'm even more impressed with the Houston lawyer. She's an extremely attractive woman, in her early thirties, tall, at least 5 feet 10 inches, slim with long slender legs, dark brown hair and a sparkling smile. I notice she wears no wedding ring. Her wide blue eyes greet me warmly as she extends her hand in a firm handshake. "Hi, I'm Carol Miller. These are my clients, Mr. and Mrs. Williams and their son Scott."

Scott's deposition doesn't take long. He's a bright teenager who responds honestly and directly to my questions. His story is basically simple.

On the morning of the accident Scott was in his room waiting for a phone call from a friend who was also vacationing on the island. The phone rang in his parent's room, which adjoined his. Upon hearing the phone, he went to his lanai, hopped over a small dividing wall to his parent's lanai and ran to answer. The next thing he remembered was waking up in the hospital with the doctors taking glass out of his arm.

Scott denied having seen decals or other markings on the glass doors prior to the accident but admitted he didn't particularly look for them either.

When questioned about baseball he testifies that he played shortstop on his freshman team with a .300 plus batting average. His coach had assured him he would make varsity in his sophomore year. Of course, once his arm was injured, his playing days were over. He's had two surgeries and a third is being scheduled. He rolls up his shirt sleeve and shows me his arm which is badly disfigured by scar tissue. I ask Scott to bend his arm and there's an obvious limitation in its range of motion.

I question him on his schooling, his grades and the courses he's taking. Scott answers not only truthfully but with enthusiasm, "Actually, this past year my grades have been better than ever. Ever since little league my only interest was baseball, but now that I can't play I've taken more of an interest in my studies and my grades have improved. Also, I've been around so many doctors lately that I'm getting interested in medicine. I'm now giving serious thought to majoring in pre-med."

The depositions of the Williams's also go smoothly. It doesn't take long to see their pride in Scott. Not only their pride, but also the horror they felt when they saw their son lying on the floor in a pool of blood surrounded by broken glass. I can feel their fear as they watched para-medics working on him, their anxiety during the hours waiting for him in the hallway of a hospital some five thousand miles from home. Within a few hours their dream vacation had turned into a nightmare as they wondered whether or not their son's arm was going to be amputated.

A Reasonable Person

They have my sympathy, but I'm in no position to help them. In fact, I'm working against their interests and feeling guilty about it. I think about how all the while they were in agony worrying about what would happen to their son, the employees of the hotel and the insurance carrier were working to prove that there was no liability on the part of the hotel. While the boy's been going through the torment of multiple surgeries, I've been part of a team preparing for the defense of a lawsuit, trying to save dollars for an insurance company.

The depositions are finished by noon and I call the hotel operator for messages. The only message is from Kathy saying she'll return after lunch giving us enough time to catch our flight to Chicago. I ask Carol if she wants to have lunch and discuss the case with me. She agrees and after saying goodbye to Scott and his parents, Carol and I go to the hotel coffee shop.

Once we're seated and order, Carol asks me how I'm enjoying Houston. I chuckle, "We got in last night about eight, took a cab from the airport, had dinner here at the hotel and we're leaving later this afternoon for Chicago. As you can see, we really won't see too much of Houston on this trip."

As iced teas are placed before us, Carol says, "I want to thank you for the way you handled my clients this morning."

"Thank me? Why?"

"You brought out all of the information quickly and smoothly, yet you were polite, respectful and even empathetic. That's unusual for a defense lawyer."

I look at her closely and see that she's sincere. "They seem like nice people and I didn't want to make this too much of an ordeal for them. What they've been going through is difficult enough." Changing the subject, I ask Carol about her law practice.

She smiles, but there is sadness in her eyes as she replies, "Well, I've been in general practice for eight years. I began right after I received my law degree from the University of Texas. I've handled just about everything, from domestic cases to general litigation and a few personal injury matters. I'd like to specialize in personal injury work, but the cases aren't too easy to get."

She pauses and regards me thoughtfully. Perhaps the empathy I seemed to exhibit with her clients prompts her to share with me more about herself. "I graduated from high school with an almost perfect 4.0 grade point average but didn't have much fun along the way. I was tall, skinny and ungainly, introverted, myopic with thick glasses and straight black hair, so not too many high school boys were interested in me. It didn't help that my parents were conservative Baptists who discouraged me from taking part in social events. In college I did somewhat better. I majored in sociology and didn't find it difficult to maintain good grades. My social life began to improve. My figure started filling out, I traded my glasses for contacts and college men began to appreciate me. But I never developed a serious relationship and decided to go to law school."

I ask, "Were there many females in law school then?"

"I read recently that almost one-third of law students in the state of Texas are female," she replies, "But when I started in 1969, the figure was half of that. Law school wasn't easy for me. Not only was the curriculum more difficult than I anticipated, but the competition was more formidable and the instructors seemed to bear down harder on females. Also, the male students weren't too friendly once they discovered I wasn't a pushover. I made friends with a few of the other students, both male and female, but was relieved when the ordeal was over and I finally graduated. I didn't make Order of the Coif but was in the top twenty-five percent of my class which was more than respectable."

"Were you offered any jobs after passing the bar?" I ask.

"Yes, with some large law firms, but it was obvious I'd be placed in a library doing nothing more than routine legal research. None of the trial firms seemed interested in me since, at that time, the general attitude was that trial work was for men only. So, I used my parents/ home as collateral, borrowed money from a local bank, rented an office and started building up a law practice. It's been long hours and hard work. It means having to take every case that walks in, coaxing other lawyers to refer cases to me, cases they weren't particularly interested in handling in the first place. But that's the way it is. I see no likelihood of being able to specialize in any particular field and bleakly picture a future of working long hours, getting old and at the end of the road winding up with a pile of paid bills."

I've been listening closely to Carol and can see what she's up against. I say, "It seems to me that general practice must be very demanding. There's too much to know and keeping up with all of the new developments is almost impossible. It's difficult enough for me to keep up with everything that's happening in my field. You must really value your independence."

She agrees. "I do enjoy my independence, but I'm paying for it by working day and night. Having no partners or associates adds to the burden. But I shouldn't complain. I make a good living and it's my choice not to work for a large firm. I enjoy helping people and most of my clients are wonderful to work with and very appreciative of what I do for them."

I think to myself how nice it would be if I had appreciative clients and tell her I envy her that part of it. We'd ordered salads and while eating, I ask, "How did you get the Williams's as clients?"

"They're friends of my sister. They're nice people. As you could tell, Scott was seriously injured."

I concur and tell her so. "There's no question about that, but I think you have a tough liability case."

Carol nods. "You may be right but Bill Peters tells me there were no warnings on the glass and it wasn't shatter proof."

I smile. "It's true the glass wasn't shatter proof but it was built pursuant to code and there were decals on the glass."

Carol shakes her head, "That's not what Peters said. He also said you have a reputation for being a good trial lawyer and a straight shooter. What are the chances of settling the case?"

I'm always pleased to hear I have a reputation for integrity and tell her so. But, I add, "I don't think the chances of settling are good. Scott's injuries are serious, and from that standpoint his case is worth a fairly substantial amount. But the insurance carrier for the hotel feels the liability picture is poor and has instructed me to proceed to trial. They may settle for a nominal sum, ten to fifteen thousand tops."

I can see that Carol is disappointed but she tries not to show it. "I know my clients won't accept that amount. They're looking for at least one hundred thousand."

Before leaving on the trip I was given authority to settle for $25,000. I then say, "If you think they would take $20,000 I'd certainly recommend it, but I'm sure my client won't go any higher."

"No! One hundred thousand is the very least they'll take. In my opinion, the case is worth more, but I've recommended one hundred thousand because of the liability factor." She looks very firm as she says this and it's difficult to tell if this is part of her negotiation strategy, a posture, or if she's being sincere. However, at this point we're so far apart in our negotiations that it doesn't matter.

I signal to the waiter for the bill and say, "Like I told you, I didn't think we'd be able to settle, but I will report your demand. However, I think your clients are being unwise. They stand a good chance of losing this case and the settlement being offered would help put Scott through college."

Carol looks almost indignant. "The boy is going to have a bad arm for the rest of his life so I really don't think $20,000 is close to compensating him."

I try to appease her, "You may be right but there's an old saying that a bad settlement is better than a good lawsuit. By the way, do you office by yourself, too?"

She answers, "Yes, I do."

"I probably shouldn't be giving advice," I say, "But it seems to me you might be better off if you enter into a loose sort of association with a number of other lawyers. You can share offices and overhead, but each has their own practice and independence. Individual lawyers that group together can specialize in areas of the law they prefer with cross-referrals between them. You would stand a better chance of being able to specialize in a field you enjoy and not have to take on so many different types of cases."

She looks at me, and it seems as if her eyes brighten. "That's not a bad idea. The approach is finding a number of other lawyers who can get along and are interested in different areas of the law. We could share rent, receptionist and equipment. Also we could have a good law library, something I certainly can't afford now."

I wonder why I seem to have a solution to everyone's' problems but my own. Why isn't there someone out there who can tell me what to do, which path to choose? I say, "My partner and I have been to many law offices around the country, and a number of lawyers are beginning to enter into that sort of arrangement. It might be much better than what you're doing now. You should give it a try."

Enthusiastically, she says, "I will. And I'm sorry we can't settle the Williams case. I'm even sorrier I won't be coming to Hawaii to try the case. I'd like to see you again and let you know how your plan is working." Looking at my wedding ring, she adds impulsively, "Why is it that every time I meet someone interesting, they're married?"

As we walk out of the coffee shop, I grin, "You shouldn't have any problems. You just need more time for your social activities. But you are good for my ego."

Carol smiles and says, "Bill Peters asked me to take the depositions of Scott's treating physicians to use at trial. I hope you'll be coming back for those."

I look at her thinking the last thing I need at this time in my life is another involvement. "No," I reply, "I don't think that would be a good idea. I'll probably send one of my associates." I don't even consider Frank.

I walk her to the entrance of the hotel and wait until a valet brings her car. I extend my hand, but she reaches over and kisses me on the cheek and says goodbye. Looking at my watch, I see it's almost time to meet Kathy for our flight to Chicago.

Chapter 29

It's almost nine the following morning as I enter a rundown brick building on Lake Shore Drive housing the court reporter's office. The lava colored bricks, many of them missing, give the appearance that the building barely survived the Chicago fire. It's not even close to having panache. As I look around I think an interior decorator would have a field day with this office. It reminds me of the offices in the elementary school I attended in Iowa. As I later tell Kathy, "It was like something out of the twilight zone, old oak desks with straight backed wooden chairs, mahogany room dividers with glass partitions and wooden file cabinets. The floor is covered with a light puke-green linoleum that curls at the edges. The receptionist desk looks like it was taken from my first grade classroom."

Since the cane backed chair behind the reception desk is empty I wander down the corridor looking for some signs of life, and finally discover an open door leading to a small conference room. Inside is an old battle-scarred oak table with six very uncomfortable looking chairs placed around it. Sitting in one of them is an angular, hawk-eyed woman in her mid-sixties. I'm surprised to see a steno machine in front of her instead of an old ink fountain pen. At least, I think to myself, she won't be asking me about job opportunities in Hawaii.

She turns out to be brisk and businesslike asking me for one of my cards and a copy of the deposition notice. She then asks about the procedure for filing depositions in Hawaii which I explain to her. I take out my file and for the next ten minutes, while waiting for the plaintiffs to arrive, read it without another word being exchanged.

A Reasonable Person

The first item I look at is the accident report. This is another case of a tourist suing a resort hotel, this one being the Lahaina Sands on Maui. From the initial report it appears to be a fairly simple slip and fall case. Mr. and Mrs. Gibson of Chicago were visiting Hawaii with one of their stops being the Lahaina Sands Hotel. On their second day Mrs. Gibson reported she fell in the bathroom, the sink having stopped up and overfilled causing the bathroom floor to be wet and slippery. Her husband called the desk clerk and an ambulance came immediately to take her to emergency at Maui Memorial Hospital, where she remained overnight so that her fractured ankle could be properly set. According to her answers to interrogatories, her ankle hasn't healed properly and is still swollen and painful.

Her attorney, Jim Green, is an experienced and shrewd lawyer who has practiced on Maui for many years. Along with the complaint he filed a request for production of documents to obtain all of the maintenance records for the Gibsons' hotel room. According to the records the room was properly maintained and there were no complaints by prior or subsequent occupants. The following day a plumber went to the room to check the sink and reported that it was functioning properly. There didn't appear to be any rational reason for the sink to overflow. Yet, when a chambermaid went to the room following the accident, the floor was soaking wet and Mrs. Gibson sustained a serious injury. I was somewhat baffled and hoped the depositions would help clear things up.

My reading is interrupted by the reporter. "It looks like we still have a little time. Would you like a cup of coffee?"

I look up, "Yes, please. Black would be fine."

She retreats from the room and within minutes returns with a large mug of coffee, saying, "I have to make a telephone call. I'll be back as soon as they get here."

As she leaves the room I take my cup to the window where there's a fabulous view of the lake. Sipping my coffee, I watch sailboats lazily tacking into the wind and my thoughts revert to Elaine.

We were next door neighbors and best friends through elementary and intermediate schools, then lovers in high school and during my first two years of community college. When I received a scholarship to the University of Arizona and told her of my plans for law school, she said she'd wait, but her waiting lasted less than a year. Following our break-up there was no contact between us for years until one morning I received a call from her.

Hearing her voice for the first time in so many years brought tears to my eyes. She kept repeating, "Are you there? Are you there?"

"Yes," I finally responded. "Where are you?"

"Home," she said. "San Rafael. I spoke to your sister and she gave me your phone number."

"My sister?" I repeated. "The next time I see that idiot I'm going to kick her ass around the block."

"Don't blame her," she laughed, "I told her it was a matter of life or death. How are you?"

I muttered, under my breath, "Probably my death." Then I replied, "I'm fine, are you okay? We haven't spoken for years, why are you calling?"

She said, "It's good hearing your voice, it's been a long time." I didn't say anything and she continued, "Are you ever in San Francisco? If so, I'd love to meet you for lunch."

She asked as if San Francisco was a short walk from Honolulu, but I replied, "Once in a while, not too often, but aren't you still married?

"I am," she answered, "But, I really want to see you. Please don't say no."

I recalled an incident that took place when we were in the second grade. She took a wild swing, giving me a bloody nose. That was the last time I ever said no to her. "Let me look at my calendar and see what I can do. I'll call you back."

Why, I wondered then, was I suddenly feeling guilty, even downright ashamed of myself? I hadn't committed myself to anything but returning her call, haven't said that I would see her. But I knew I would do whatever she asked me. The good angel who was telling me that I was free to refuse her was being stifled by my old self, the one who would always be in bondage to her will. The feelings aroused by the sound of her voice had already dictated what I would do. And what about Kathy? How would I look her in the eye? I had every reason to refuse to meet Elaine again, but I knew from the outset that reasons wouldn't be enough to resist her.

That was five years ago, and I was still in bondage to Elaine. Looking Kathy in the eye wasn't hard for me as long as I was able to conceal my double life. I could never tell her the truth. The truth will make you free, so it's said. But the truth is that a woman can never forgive when she's been betrayed. So I had opted to live a lie, letting her believe I was a faithful loving mate. But now Elaine was forcing me to choose.

I don't have much time to dwell on my predicament or how I got into it. The pressures of the moment impinge as people enter the room, and I think to myself, "Here we go again." It takes me less than two hours to depose the Gibsons. I leave to meet Kathy for lunch.

Entering the small Italian café recommended by the concierge, I look around, but Kathy hasn't arrived yet. I'm seated at a comfortable booth, and order a vodka tonic for Kathy. I settle for a beer.

Spotting Kathy as she enters, I wave her over and rise to give her a kiss. She looks wonderful in egg shell white pants and a pink sleeveless top. My shirt is still sticky from the August humidity, but Kathy looks like she's been sitting in air conditioning all morning.

She picks up her drink, saying, "It's really hot out. Thanks for ordering a drink for me." She takes a sip which wouldn't quench the thirst of a sparrow, leans back and sighs, "That's good."

Half of my beer disappears in one gulp as the waiter approaches for our orders. Kathy requests a small caesar salad, I ask for spaghetti with meat sauce. Kathy takes another taste of her drink, asking, "How did your depositions go?"

"It was somewhat odd." I answer, and continue, "Not the people. They seem nice enough, early sixties, neat and clean looking. This was their first trip to Hawaii. It's the case that's odd. I can't believe they're actually pursuing it." I guzzle down some more beer.

Kathy asks, "What happened?"

I smile, thinking of their testimony. "Mrs. Gibson testified that after lunch they went for a walk on the beach, returning to the hotel after an hour or so. She decided to take a nap and lay down on the bed. She awoke, went into the bathroom and slipped on the wet floor. Her injuries appear to be serious and permanent.

The waiter brings our food. Mine looks absolutely mouth-watering. Between bites, I continue, "Mr. Gibson testified that during their walk he collected a number of sea shells for his granddaughter. He said there were about a dozen nice sized shells that he wrapped in a towel to bring back to their room.

Kathy interrupts, "Are you going to eat all of that. It's a lot of food."

I take a big forkful of the pasta and say, "I'm starving, I didn't have any breakfast." I then go on, "He went on to say that after his wife was asleep, he took the shells into the bathroom and put them in the sink to wash off the sand. He left the water running on them and went out to the lanai to read."

"You mean to say," Kathy exclaims, "The entire time she was asleep he let the water run. No wonder the sink overflowed."

"Exactly," I say. "I asked him why he was suing the hotel. He said that his lawyer told him he had a good case because the overflow valve should have drained off the water."

Kathy shakes her head. "I'm no plumber, but I don't think so."

"I don't either," I reply. "Neither did the Chicago lawyer who was there for Jim Green. He simply shrugged his shoulders in a gesture of disbelief. Later, the court reporter said it was absurd."

Kathy says, "I'm certain she's seen more than her share of absurd cases. What are you going to do about this one?"

"When we return," I reply, "I'll see if Jim Green will settle for his costs. He's smart and must realize how silly the case is. If not, I think it would be a good one for David to try. I'm sure Ventura will agree."

"That's a good idea. The younger people should be trying some of them."

I frown. "I've been working on that but the companies insist that Frank or I try the cases." I finish my lunch and note that Kathy has half of her salad left. I motion for the waiter to bring the bill and tell Kathy, "I'm stuffed, let's go back to our hotel. I can use a nap."

Kathy has an I told you so look but, kindly, says nothing as we leave the restaurant.

CHAPTER 30

Later that evening, after dinner, we find a comfortable booth in the cocktail lounge of our hotel. Kathy asks, "What's your deposition about tomorrow?"

"It's somewhat of an unusual situation," I answer. "It's one of Frank's cases. From what he told me it's a fairly routine rear-ender that took place on Maui, a typical fender bender. The plaintiff is claiming a classic neck strain, whiplash injury. She was working part-time as a cocktail waitress and claimed that following the accident she was unable to work for several months. She took chiropractic treatments and massage therapy for her neck. We must have dozens of cases like this. The insurance companies settle the vast majority of them rather than have to pay the costs of going to trial.

"At any rate," I continue, "Frank took the deposition of the plaintiff about six months ago. She testified her neck pain was excruciating, she was off work for months and still couldn't participate in any of her normal activities.

Prior to the accident she jogged, rode her bike, played volleyball at the beach and generally led a very active life. Now she claims that she can't do any of those activities. Oh yes, she also testified she hasn't been able to engage in sex because it makes her neck hurt even more."

Kathy laughs, "What can she do? Sit in the corner and knit?"

I smile, "We see so many of these cases we do get cynical. The problem is that many of them are genuine. But since the injuries are mainly subjective, it's difficult to prove which ones are authentic and which ones are not. She said all she could do was sit around watching TV propped up so her neck wouldn't hurt. She only left the house to go for chiropractic treatments and massage therapy."

Kathy asks, "Who pays for all of that?"

"Hawaii's a no fault state, so her insurance company has to pay her medical bills and loss of earnings."

Kathy is skeptical, "So she's paid for staying off work and gets her medical bills taken care of until her no fault benefits run out?"

"Exactly."

Kathy looks at me in surprise, "Then she settles with the other person's insurance carrier?"

"Correct, as long as her bills are over a certain amount."

Kathy now seems annoyed, "Sounds like a racket to me."

I reply, "Not always. There are a number of people who really are injured. Whiplash can be a serious problem. The difficulty is distinguishing the real cases from the phonies. But we may have got some help in this case."

Kathy appears puzzled, "How?"

"The insurance company received a letter from a woman named Helen Wilson. Apparently she was the plaintiff's roommate at the time of the accident. Helen said the plaintiff is the biggest phony she's ever met. She was constantly bragging about how she was going to swindle the insurance company and told Helen that even though she hadn't really been hurt she was going to take off work for several months because she was advised it would help her case. During that time the plaintiff jogged on a daily basis, continued to play volleyball and engaged in all of her usual activities. Also, on numerous occasions during this period, she brought men home to spend the night with her." I add sarcastically, "Of course, they could have been giving her massage therapy."

Kathy smiles, "Does this happen very often?"

"Unfortunately for us, this is very rare. It happens once in a while but normally the letter writer is anonymous or turns out to be some kind of flake or disgruntled lover or former spouse. Someone who's out for revenge. But this woman seems legitimate. She had a one year contract with Maui Community College teaching some specialized nursing courses and is now head surgical nurse at St. Michael's hospital here in Chicago. Frank spoke to her and said she sounded fine but couldn't return to Maui for the trial so would have to be deposed here."

Kathy smiles, "At least it looks like this is one phony who won't get away with it." She yawns, "I'm tired. It's been a long day. Let's go to bed."

The following morning I again decide to walk to the court reporter's office. It's a beautiful morning with blue, cloudless skies and a warm wind drifting across the lake. Usually this time of year is hot and humid but this is a perfect day for walking. There aren't many pedestrians out and many of them are casual and friendly, nodding and sometimes even waving to me as they pass.

Even the reporters' offices seem brighter this morning. There's still no one sitting at the receptionist desk, so again I walk down the hall to the conference room. The room is empty but the steno machine is set up in its usual place and there's a carafe of hot coffee on the table along with some cups. I pour a cup and sit down patiently waiting for the witness and the other attorney to appear.

The first person through the door is Helen Wilson. To say she's big would be an understatement. Maybe she's not quite large enough to play middle linebacker for the Chicago Bears, but she's as square as a crate with immense shoulders and arms. A scarlet colored caftan, which does nothing to conceal her bulk, comes down to her sandals, which look like two small canoes. Her body is gross, but she has a pleasant, intelligent face with alert and expressive eyes.

She sticks out her hand and greets me, "Are you Mr. Cooper?"

I smile, thinking to myself that once again Cooper has lucked out by ducking this deposition, "No, I'm Mark Dorsey, Mr. Cooper's partner. Are you Helen Wilson?"

Her voice is surprisingly soft and sensual. "Yes, I am. I thought Mr. Cooper would be here."

"Sorry, he couldn't make it, but since I was planning on being in Chicago he asked me to handle this deposition for him."

Frank must have been exceptionally charming on the phone. She looks disappointed, but shrugs stoically and says, "I guess it's all right. When do we start?" She then adds, "Do you have any special instructions for me?"

I tell her we'll get started as soon as the other attorney arrives. I then tell her, "It's a simple procedure. I'll ask you questions concerning Joan Miller and all you have to do is tell the truth. After I'm through, the other attorney may have some questions. Again, just tell the truth and everything will be fine. If you don't know an answer just say so. Please don't guess at any answers."

As I'm telling her this, a man in his middle sixties enters the room wearing a wrinkled navy blue, shiny gabardine leisure suit and a light brown sport shirt open at the neck. It looks like the entire outfit was bought at Goodwill along with the bulky briefcase he's carrying. His manner is brusque and officious as he asks me, "Are you Cooper?"

I answer, "No. I'm Mark Dorsey, Cooper's partner. I'll be taking the deposition."

He practically barks at me, "My name is Stevens. I've been retained by Hawaii counsel to represent the plaintiff for the deposition. Why did you schedule it so early?"

I apologize, "I'm sorry, but I have to leave for Toronto this afternoon and this was the only way I could work it into my schedule."

Helen then interrupts, "Besides, I requested it for this time. I have to be at work later this morning."

The court reporter enters the room, sits down at her machine and looks around with the same hawklike eyes to see if we're ready to proceed. We are, although Stevens still looks irritated.

After Helen is sworn in, I ask her some preliminary questions establishing her address, age and marital status. In a straightforward manner she answers that she is 34, lives in Chicago, has never been married and was given a one year contract to teach two specialized courses in surgical nursing at Maui Community College. She rented a small two bedroom house in the Kihei section of Maui and advertised for a roommate.

The first person to answer the ad was Joan Miller, an attractive young woman of 29. Joan said she didn't smoke or drink and was interested in saving money at her waitress job in order to return to San Diego and buy a small condo for herself. At the time, she looked like the perfect roommate.

It didn't take long for Helen to learn the truth. Joan returned home every night after work with a different man, would turn up the stereo until the house shook and stayed up most nights listening to music and smoking marijuana. At times, the smell of pot was almost strong enough to even get Helen high as she lay awake behind the closed door of her bedroom.

Helen testifies that strangely enough the situation got worse after the accident. Joan refused to go to work, admitting to Helen the only reason she didn't work was to help her case. She went jogging every morning before her chiropractor appointments. As soon as she returned from the chiropractor she would engage in her daily volleyball game on the beach. Joan's nightly activities continued with as much intensity as before the accident. In short, according to Helen, Joan engaged in more physical activities after the accident than before, which would lead anyone to the obvious conclusion that she definitely was not injured as a result of her auto accident.

I finish questioning her and ask Stevens if he wishes to examine the witness.

Stevens starts by practically shouting at Helen, "Isn't it true you were jealous of Miss Miller and hated her because she had boyfriends and you didn't?"

Helen calmly answers, "Absolutely not. I was angry at her because she made so much noise, smoked pot in my house, brought all kinds of strange men home and obviously was a liar and a cheat."

Infuriated by her cool rebuttal, Stevens, tries to provoke her. "Isn't it true that you're a lesbian and became angry at Joan because she rejected your sexual advances to her?"

Unprovoked, Helen merely smiles, "Make up your mind. Did I hate her because she had boyfriends and I didn't or because I'm a lesbian and she rejected my advances? I don't think you can have it both ways."

Stevens ignores her reply and asks, "Isn't it true that you beat her up and as a result the police were called to the house and arrested you?"

Helen andwers, "No. That's not quite what happened."

"Well, what happened?" Stevens demands.

"I told her that I thought what she was doing was wrong. She said she was only trying to get money out of a rich insurance company and she saw nothing wrong with that. I told her she was a liar and a cheat and I threw her out of the house along with her clothes. The police were called, questioned us, said it was not a police matter and left. That was the last time I saw her."

Stevens then makes what I consider one of the biggest blunders a lawyer can make in questioning a witness. He asks Helen, "By the way, I saw you talking to Mr. Dorsey as I was entering the room. Did he tell you what to say?"

Helen: "Yes."

Stevens: "What did he tell you to say?"

Helen: "He told me to tell the truth."

Stevens turns red and says he has no further questions. I ask Helen, "Did Joan actually admit she was trying to swindle the insurance carrier?"

Helen answers, "Yes. On several occasions she told me the only reason she stayed off work and went for therapy was to swindle money out of the insurance company."

The deposition is concluded and Stevens rushes out without a word.

I thank Helen. "I realize it was difficult for you but we really do appreciate your helping us like this."

Helen shakes hands and after she leaves I turn to the reporter and ask, "What do you think of that one?"

The reporter answers, "I think you're lucky she came forward. That doesn't happen too often."

I agree, say goodbye and start my walk back to the hotel. The flight to Toronto won't leave for several hours. Entering the cocktail lounge of a small hotel, I order a draft beer and look around. The room is empty except for the bartender. As I sip my beer, I think of Elaine. At moments like this, when I'm undistracted, I can see things clearly and face some demoralizing truths.

I'm infatuated with Elaine but I realize that my infatuation is bound up with the memory of who we were so many years ago. Then we were like young animals playing in a forest oblivious to the world outside. It's the same now when I'm with her. While I'm with her, I'm freed of all the problems and pressures of my daily life, running free in a forest. It's been said that when you're in love with someone, you're also in love with how you see yourself in relation to that person. With Elaine I'm a free spirit, unburdened by guilt or obligation, and while we're together I become who I was when we were young.

I'm always under her spell, but at moments like this I'm able to see clearly that my feelings for Elaine are based more on fantasy than reality, that I'm really in love with a dream, the dream we live in our moments together.

The reality I can't escape is that I'm betraying the trust of another woman I love, Kathy, my wife of twelve years. I order another beer and think of Kathy. She's everything a man could want a wife to be – beautiful, intelligent, loving and gifted with a great sense of humor. Also, she has been wonderful with my daughters who consider her their true mother. We've been a good family with love, affection, friendship and closeness. This is reality.

It occurs to me that my yearning to escape with Elaine may be partly rooted in how I've come to see myself professionally, as nothing more than a hired gun paid to shoot it out in a courtroom. Running away with Elaine could mean casting off this role I've found downright hateful at times, being compelled to serve a system that is grossly unfair. A look at the cases of just the past few days is enough to show the unfairness of the system. Some cases where people are badly hurt but receive no compensation.

Others where the people may be complete phonies and hit pay dirt. What happened to the truth and justice discussed so much in law school? I ask myself. That lasted until the first day of your first job after passing the bar exam. What it all boils down to is winning or, as in the case of most trial lawyers including myself, the hatred of losing.

Deep down I believe that running off with Elaine and playing in the forest for the rest of our lives is an unrealistic fantasy, but could it really happen? Would it be so terrible for us to leave and live for ourselves? Or is it just another daydream? We've missed every chance up to now, but time is running out on us. There aren't going to be many chances left, I'm going to have to make a decision.

But, I think, 'Not today. No decisions today.' I leave the bar and walk back to my hotel not particularly looking forward to the next few days in Toronto.

CHAPTER 31

I'm back in Honolulu and looking forward to Sings noodles. It's not even noon and the restaurant is already packed. As usual, the noise is deafening and, as usual, we almost have to yell to be heard. As I start stuffing myself with noodles, Frank asks, "How did your depositions go?"

In between bites I tell him about Helen Wilson. "She was an excellent witness and came over as extremely sincere and truthful. You may get a defense verdict with her testimony."

Frank asks, "What did she look like?"

I answer, "Pretty, but a little on the heavy side."

Frank smiles and then asks, "How was Toronto? I've always wanted to go there."

As I start to answer, David and Julie arrive and place their orders. I say to them, "Frank asked me about Toronto. Have either of you been there?"

They both shake their heads.

I tell them, "Kathy and I really enjoyed it. Toronto is a beautiful city. It has wide, clean streets with a variety of ethnic neighborhoods and yet has somewhat of a British feel to it. We had a tour of the courthouse and the lawyers still wear robes and wigs. Two of the depositions were in a small town about two hours out of the city. It was a spectacular drive with Lake Ontario on one side and dozens of small lakes on the other."

Frank asks, "What's the case about?"

Julie had attended the depositions of our client and says, "A woman was hurt on an escalator at the airport. Apparently a young boy caught his pants leg on the side of the escalator steps. This caused a bottleneck at

A Reasonable Person

the bottom and the people turned around and tried to go back up. In the confusion the plaintiff was knocked down and injured. We represent the company which maintains the escalator."

David asks, "What's the plaintiff's theory of liability?"

Julie responds, "If I recall correctly their theory is fairly simple. If the escalator had been properly designed it would have been almost impossible for the boy to have caught his pants leg in it. In that case the only reason the pants leg could get caught would be because of improper maintenance."

I continue, "According to the maintenance manual the escalator is designed with a $3/8^{th}$ of an inch gap between the steps and the side. As part of their regular maintenance routine our client measures the gap to ensure that it doesn't vary from that figure. If it's narrower, the steps rub against the side. If it's wider, items can get entangled in it."

Julie adds as I inhale more noodles, "When the escalator was inspected immediately after the accident the gap was exactly 3/8ths of an inch wide. However, the escalator company has hired an expert who will testify that with a gap of 3/8ths of an inch there's no way the pants leg could have been caught. It's our theory that since the maintenance company acted reasonably in following the manual that there's no negligence on its part."

"I agree," but add, "However, the case does have a humorous side to it which was revealed at the depositions."

They stop eating and look at me. Frank asks, "What's that?"

I reply, "According to the witnesses the boy did catch his pants leg about half-way down the escalator. Meanwhile at the bottom, a woman dropped a cake. Apparently it was a birthday cake she had made and brought from Canada for her sister. The cake was splattered at the bottom of the escalator and the people were trying to step around or over it as the boy reached the bottom. Between the cake and the stuck boy people started to turn around and go back up the escalator. The plaintiff saw people coming back towards her so she turned around to go up and that's when she fell injuring her knee."

Frank bursts out laughing. "That's hard to believe. A woman brings a cake all the way from Canada and then drops it at the bottom of the escalator! That must have been one hell of a scene. What a way to start a Hawaiian vacation."

David is also laughing. "Then some kid's pants leg is stuck. What caused the panic, the pants or the cake?"

I say, "None of the witnesses could answer that, but I agree it must have been one hell of a scene. However, the plaintiff did have surgery on her knee, though it seems to be fine now." I finish my noodles.

Frank looks at me. "I hear you have a trial starting tomorrow on Maui. What's that about?"

I pour fresh cups of tea and between sips reply, "It's a wrongful death case. A truck driver was electrocuted on our client's construction site. We represent the general contractor."

David finishes for me, "I took some of the Maui depositions on that case. If I remember correctly, he was driving a large truck and the top of the cab came into contact with a high voltage wire that was hanging too low over the construction site."

I say, "That's right. Our client sent a number of messages to the electric company asking them to remove the wire as it could be dangerous. Unfortunately, the electric company did nothing. Naturally they're also a party to the case. Hopefully the jury will assess most of the liability to it."

Frank asks, "Any chance of settlement?"

"I finish my tea. "I don't think so. The demand is too high and the electric company insists that we pay 50% of any settlement. I think we'll do better in trial."

David asks, "Will you need any assistance on Maui. I'd love to go."

I smile, "Not really. From my standpoint the trial won't be difficult. I'll just keep pointing my finger at the electric company. I normally hate being in the position of fighting a co-defendant rather than the plaintiff, but I don't have a choice in this case."

Frank adds, "Don't you have any chance of getting some comparative negligence on the part of the driver?"

I answer, "Very little, if any. According to witnesses he opened the door screaming that his truck was on fire. If he had jumped clear he would have been alright. But as he stepped out of the truck he kept holding on to the door so when he touched the ground ....."

"Zap! He was immediately grounded." Frank finishes my sentence.

I grimace, "Is 'zap' some sort of engineering term?"

David smiles. "I don't think I'd use a technical term like that to the jury."

I reply sarcastically, "I'll try to avoid it. I think the jury will be sympathetic enough as it is. I'll let the electric company argue comparative negligence. I'll confine my arguments to putting all the blame on the electric company for not removing the wire even though asked many times to do so."

As usual I pick up the check before returning to the office.

Chapter 32

It's Monday evening and I've returned from my Maui electrocution case. Everyone except Frank and I have left for the day. I'm sitting in Frank's office watching him fill my glass with a fine looking purple liquid. I take a sip and ask, "Okay, I give. What is it?"

Frank smiles and with an affected British accent answers, "This, my best friend and esteemed partner, is one of the finest port wines money can buy. I bought it at a small shop outside of London a few years ago, and even I am too embarrassed to tell you how much I paid."

I laugh, "Does that mean I should sip and not gulp?"

Frank grimaces. "If you gulp this finest of all ports you will be shot at sunrise."

Keeping a close eye on Frank I carefully sip the wine. From what I can tell, it could have cost two dollars a bottle but that may be due to my mid-western taste buds. Nonetheless, I put what I hope is an ecstatic look on my face and say, "What a great wine! What are we celebrating?"

Frank smiles. "I knew you'd love it. We both got defense verdicts today and my divorce was finalized. Excellent reasons to celebrate. Did your trial go smoothly?"

"Yes," I answer, "Actually it did except for one incident. Bob Greenwood represented the electric company. As you know he can be sort of feisty at times."

Frank grins. "I know. I worked for him when I first passed the bar. He can be difficult to say the least."

I continue. "One of my key witnesses had left the state before the trial. Bob and I previously agreed that I could use his deposition at trial without the necessity of going through the charade of issuing a subpoena for him."

Frank groans. "I hope you had it in writing."

I nod. "Absolutely. I sent him a confirming letter at the time. But, when I submitted the deposition, he objected on the grounds that there was no proof that the witness was unavailable. I brought out the letter and the judge overruled his objection and allowed the deposition to be read to the jury."

Frank says, "Sounds right to me."

"At the noon recess, after the courtroom cleared, Bob came over to me and said that he didn't appreciate what I had done."

Frank looks bewildered. "What did you do wrong?"

"He claimed that it made him look like a liar to the judge. He said to me and I quote, 'I should bust you in the chops!'"

Frank bursts out laughing. "He said what?"

I start laughing too. "You heard me. He said he would bust me in the chops. I haven't heard that expression for years. It absolutely left me speechless."

Frank stops laughing. "I always knew he was an ass, but that's over the top even for him. What did you do?"

"After getting my composure back, I told him that if he 'busted me in the chops' I would sue him and end up with his Rolls Royce. He countered by saying he had ample insurance to pay for the horrific injuries he was about to inflict upon me. I reminded him that insurance doesn't cover intentional acts."

Frank starts laughing again. "So instead of fighting you got into a coverage dispute?"

I smile and hold out my glass for some more of the port. "Much more lawyerlike, right? We went to lunch so we could discuss it further and he finally agreed that since there was no insurance coverage he wouldn't hit me. Another funny thing happened."

Frank fills my glass. "Why are my trials so dull. Tell me."

"Our foreman testified that when the cab of the truck struck the hot wire, he was on the bed of the truck. He saw what happened and could see the tires smoking. He knew that if he tried to climb off of the truck he'd be electrocuted so he took about ten steps back and then ran and took a flying leap off the truck. He testified that if jumping off the back of trucks was an Olympic event he'd have won the gold. Fortunately, he only ended up with a sprained ankle."

We are both laughing now. Frank asks, "What was the final award?"

I answer, "As you know they found no negligence on the part of my client. They found the electric company 100% negligent with no comparative on the part of the driver and the total award amounted to about $750,000. Greenwood was fuming. I quickly left before he changed his mind and busted me in the chops. How did your trial go?" I didn't have to ask him about his divorce. The only assets he has left are his partnership interest in our law firm and a photo of his new girlfriend on his desk.

He shrugs. "It went smoothly. An elderly female tourist slipped and fell at the Beach Hotel. The janitors had just washed down the tile floor and it was still wet as she was rushing to the breakfast buffet."

I ask, "Did they have any signs up?"

Frank nods, "They had so many warning signs it was a wonder she didn't trip over one of them. Naturally she denied seeing any."

I take another sip of the port. It's starting to taste better. I ask, "Was she seriously injured?"

Frank replies, "Yes. Her hip had been replaced about fifteen years before the accident and the fall dislocated her hip so she needed a new replacement."

Taking another sip of Frank's port, I think to myself that I could easily get addicted to this stuff. "I thought hip replacements only lasted for about fifteen years."

Frank nods. "That's right. I took her doctor,s deposition and he testified that even without the fall she was due for a new hip. He further testified that following the new replacement she has been doing better than before the fall." He then adds, "By the way she was from Naples, Florida, and that's where I took his deposition."

Never having been there I ask, "How was Naples?"

Frank smiles. "It's a beautiful area. I sat on the balcony of my hotel watching the sun set over the Gulf. It was breathtaking. However, I think it has more golf courses than people and when I asked my waitress what Naples was all about she told me it was about hordes of mid-westerners flooding the town during the winter months. A nice place to visit." He then adds, "Don't you have a trial starting tomorrow?"

I nod, "Yes. Another stupid case. The plaintiff was seen staggering to his car at Paradise Park, the bird sanctuary at the top of Manoa. The accident occurred about one mile down the hill. The plaintiff, trying to negotiate a curve, drove on the wrong side of the road hitting an on coming

Hawaiian Adventure tour bus head-on. The plaintiff was seriously injured. Both legs and two ribs broken."

Frank asks, "How do you place him on the wrong side of the road?"

"I answer, "Aside from the bus driver there are two neighbors who after hearing the crash immediately rushed to the scene. Both will testify that the plaintiff's vehicle was on the wrong side. In addition, there's the police report done by the officers who arrived on the scene. It clearly shows that the plaintiff was on the wrong side. I took the deposition of the plaintiff and he remembers nothing about the accident."

Frank shakes his head in disbelief. "Who's the plaintiff's attorney and what's his theory on liability?"

"Frank Choi represents him and I don't have a clue as to what his theory is."

Frank finishes his wine and says, "Choi is as dumb as he is arrogant. It should be an easy winner." As he says this the phone rings, which is unusual since it's after seven.

Frank pushes the speaker button and says "Hello."

A voice, which I easily recognize as Elaine's, comes through his speaker phone. "Hello. Is Mr. Dorsey there? Please tell him Elaine is calling."

I tell Frank I'll talk to her in my office. Frank gives me a questioning look and asks, "Who's that?" I tell him it's a client but he's too smart for that. I can almost feel his smirk boring into my back as I leave the room.

Chapter 33

It's Friday afternoon and once again I'm in Frank's office. We're celebrating my win in the Paradise Park case but this time with a glass of brandy. I think to myself that if I don't stop winning cases I'll end up an alcoholic.

I'm telling Frank about the outcome of my case when David enters and sits. I continue. "After we both rested I made a motion for a directed verdict. Judge Azeka asked Choi if he admitted that the plaintiffs vehicle had crossed over to the opposite lane and hit the bus head-on. Choi said there was no dispute as to that."

Frank asks, "So what was his theory?"

I say, "That's exactly what the judge asked him. Choi said that since it was a dangerous road with so many curves that the bus company should have an assistant on the bus. As the bus approaches a curve it should come to a complete stop. The assistant should get out on the road to warn on-coming vehicles that the bus is about to round the corner."

Both Frank and David start laughing. David utters, "He had to be kidding. That's one of the stupidest things I've ever heard."

I also laugh. "That's exactly what the judge said as he granted my motion and dismissed the case. He added that it wasn't worthy enough to go to the jury."

David says that he wants to discuss the case we have scheduled for Monday. Frank says to David, "Can you discuss it later? I have to talk to Mark for a moment. Please close the door."

David nods and leaves the room. Frank takes a sip of his brandy and then says, "Who is Elaine?"

I answer. "A friend."

Frank raises his voice. "Bullshit! Who is she?"

I try to remain calm. "I don't know if that's any of your business."

Frank stands, walks around his desk and sits in the other clients' chair. "Mark," he says, "We've been friends for over eleven years. There's never been the slightest rumor about you being unfaithful to Kathy. Not once has it entered my mind that you might be unfaithful, not until the other night when Elaine called. None of our clients ever call after business hours. You know, I'd do anything for you so if there's anything I can do please let me know."

I think that it would feel good to be able to talk to someone about it. I finish my brandy, and say, "Alright, I'll tell you about it. But it has to be just between the two of us."

Frank sits back. "Of course."

I lean back in my chair and tell Frank the entire story. I add, "Now that she's getting a divorce she told me that we can't go on the way we have been."

Frank has been surprisingly quiet as I spoke but now he asks, "Have you said anything about this to Kathy?"

"Absolutely not!" I snap, and then continue. "Frank, from the time I first met Kathy, I've never been seriously tempted by another woman. I've been completely faithful, except for Elaine of course."

Frank shakes his head and says, "If Kathy knew any of this it would break her heart."

"I know," I reply. I can't even express the guilt that I feel over this. Sometimes I can't even look Kathy in the eye I feel so bad. But when it comes to Elaine I can't seem to help myself. It's like being under a spell, a spell that I can't rid myself of."

Frank says, "You realize that if you lose Kathy you'll also lose most of your friends? Not me, of course, but most of them would side with her."

"I know that," I reply, "but my main concern is Kathy. The thought of hurting her breaks my heart."

"Then don't," he says. "What you have with her is the kind of relationship I would give anything to have. I had it with Donna and might have had it with Lynn before things started going to hell between us. Now I have no one. Believe me, you'll regret it if you lose Kathy. Whatever you have with Elaine just isn't worth it. You've got to break it off with her. That would be the right thing to do."

I almost have to laugh thinking since when has Frank ever done the right thing. But, I reply, "If only it were that easy."

As though he's heard what I'm thinking, he answers, "Christ knows, I've done the wrong thing often enough, and I'm feeling the consequences. That's why I'm trying to make you see what's at stake. You don't have to make the same mistakes I did."

He pauses a moment to let this sink in. Then he goes on, "You know, Mark, "I suspect that a big part of Elaine's attraction for you is that she represents an escape from this ratrace we're both caught up in, using our so-called trial skills to see that people who are seriously injured walk away with nothing or very little. Trying to save wealthy insurance companies a few dollars. Not even to mention the fact that it's a grind. We're either in trial or preparing for trial. I get sick and tired of it and I'm sure you do too. Most of the time I find it difficult to believe that this is why we went to law school. You don't really want to leave Kathy, but you're fed up and ready to jettison all the bullshit."

"Yes," I have to agree. "There are times when it really gets to me. But, I guess it beats sitting at a desk writing contracts all day, and these fat insurance companies do pay our bills. There are many days when I feel like just walking away from it all."

Frank nods and says, " But you need to see what's really driving you. It strikes me that you're in love with a dream. Having a two or three times a year affair is a lot different than living with her day in and day out. And she surely isn't going to make it any easier for you to deal with all the crap and craziness that goes on around here.

What he says makes sense. The fact that he himself hasn't shown much good judgment in matters of the heart doesn't invalidate his argument. I reply, "You may be right, and I appreciate your input. I just need to think about what I'm going to do. "Meanwhile, I don't have to make a decision today."

Frank comes over and shakes my hand. "I'm sure you'll give it very serious thought but remember that no matter what you decide we'll still be friends, no matter what happens I'll be behind you."

"I know that, Frank," I say as I leave the room've never doubted that," I say, as I leave the room. "And I'm damned grateful."

I return to my office and get David on the intercom. "Please come in and bring me a cup of coffee."

Gazing out the window, I watch two Phantom Jets climb into the sky at what seems like breathtaking speed. Within moments they're out of sight. David enters with a large file in one hand and a cup of coffee in the other.

I let out a huge groan. "Well, what the hell is next weeks trial about?"

PART 3

AUGUST, 1981

CHAPTER 34

It's Saturday morning and I've been on the phone with Elaine for almost an hour. She's pleasant but direct. Her divorce has been final for months and she's pressuring me to make a decision. I agree but tell her that I start trial on Monday and have two more trials back to back following that one. She tells me I have to fish or cut bait, whatever that means. We say goodbye. There's no time to think about what I'm going to do. Fish or cut bait? I need to think about it, but now is not the time.

Frank walks in holding a cup of coffee and sprawls out on my couch. He asks, "What's happening?"

I answer, "Not much. I have three trials back to back and it doesn't seem as if any will settle. Trying to juggle witnesses is a bitch. Oh yes, I just got off the phone with Elaine. What does 'fish or cut bait' mean?"

Frank laughs. "Damned if I know. I would think that literally it means to either do something new and productive or keep on doing what you've been doing."

David enters the room and I ask him the meaning of the phrase. He responds, "Isn't it the same as 'put up or shut up?' In other words, make up your damn mind."

Frank says, "Yes, something like 'shit or get off the pot.' What's your trial about on Monday?"

"Some kid went through the lanai door of his hotel room at the Kona Beach Hotel. His arm was almost severed but he seems to be doing alright now."

Frank asks. "Were there decals on the door?"

David answers. "The hotel employees sealed off the room and had a photographer there immediately after the accident."

I reach into a folder and bring out six large photos depicting a shattered glass door with a number of decals still adhered to it. "Look at these. It clearly shows decals on what remains of the door."

Frank takes the photos, looks at them and says, "No question about it. The door was plastered with decals. So what's their theory?"

I respond. "They claim the glass should have been shatter proof, but the hotel was built according to code and the code wasn't changed until long after it was constructed."

David says, "Under the revised code any replacement doors must be shatter proof. However, the new code doesn't apply to existing glass doors."

Frank yawns. "It should be a defense verdict, but you never know what those Big Island jurors will do. I assume it will be tried in Hilo."

"I say, "You're right on both counts. It will be tried in Hilo and there will be a lot of sympathy for the kid. He's a nice appearing young man who'll be a good witness on his own behalf. He wanted to be a major league baseball player and that dream has been squashed."

Frank scoffs. "We all wanted to be major league baseball players and look where we've ended up. Who's his lawyer?"

I reply, "Bill Peters from Kona. He seems like a nice guy, but their Houston lawyer was a real knockout. She could have been Miss Texas."

David nods his head. "That's very true. I attended the depositions of his Houston doctors and I couldn't take my eyes off of her legs."

I smile, "No wonder legs were mentioned so often in the depositions."

Frank laughs. "It sounds more like a beauty contest than depositions. You should've had me go."

I've noted that for several months there have been no pictures of girlfriends adorning his desk. I say, "If you had been there you'd have given her your entire stash of macadamia nuts." Frank is well known for filling his briefcase with packages of Hawaiian macadamias' to take on deposition trips. According to him they're great ice breakers.

Frank gets up and stretches. "If I had been there I would have settled the case with her over a nice glass of wine."

It's my turn to laugh. "I tried to settle the case with her over a romantic lunch and a nice glass of iced tea. She's as tough as she is pretty."

A Reasonable Person

As Frank walks out of the room he says, "You must be losing your charm, if you ever had any. Thank God I still have mine."

I yell out, "Bullshit!" but he's already closed the door.

I turn to David who has a big smile. "It looks like the Williams case is under control," I tell him. "I fly to Hilo tomorrow afternoon. If all goes smoothly it should finish Friday. After that is the escalator case. Please make sure that it's ready to go. You can second chair me."

David looks pleased. "Thanks. That's an interesting case. I'll review and outline all of the depositions. It'll be ready." He gets up to leave.

A thought occurs to me and I ask David to have a seat. "David," I say, "I'm a little concerned about Frank. He hasn't seemed to be himself recently. Have you noticed anything?"

"Well, now that you mention it, I've noticed that he doesn't seem to be himself," David replies. "He hasn't for several months. I know he broke up with his girlfriend. I think he's been under a lot of pressure lately. He's had one long trial after another, and they seem to have taken a lot out of him."

I frown. "He's always been up for long trials, able to take them in stride. That sort of thing never bothered him before. Maybe I should have a talk with him."

In fact, I need someone to have a talk with me. Not Frank, of course. He's already told me what I should do about Elaine. I need someone who really understands how I feel and what I'm up against.

I pick up my folders and head for the door. "Thanks for your input, David. See you next Saturday." I leave the office and drive home, where the person who understands me best is waiting, the one person I can't turn to now for help with what's really weighing on me.

Once home I quickly strip down to a bathing suit and join Kathy in our pool. It must be over eighty degrees out and the pool feels incredible. Not being much of a swimmer, I lounge in the shallow end cooling off. Kathy looks absolutely striking as she swims slow, graceful laps. As I watch her I feel myself being torn in two. Frank is right. She is a gem. How can I really be thinking of leaving her?

Kathy glides softly through the water and spreads out next to me. Her breathing is deep but easy. She starts massaging my neck and says, "Lately you've been acting as if something serious has been bothering you. Can you tell me what's on your mind?"

I shake my head. "Same old thing. Too many trials, trying to run a law firm, not enough hours in the day. I think this is the first time I've been in the pool all summer."

She nods. "I think you're right, but it seems as if something else is bothering you. I wish you'd tell me what it is."

I wonder to myself if it's that obvious to everyone, but I say, "No. There's really nothing else. Sometimes I feel that we should take leaves of absence for a year and get the hell out of here."

Kathy sits up and looks at me. "Are you serious? I'd love it. The thought of spending a year with you away from your rat race is absolutely enchanting. We could easily rent out this place for a year. We could find a place in Europe - France, Italy, Switzerland. Maybe Spain."

I interrupt. "Maybe we can sell everything. The house, my practice, everything and then get the hell out of here permanently."

Kathy looks at me dubiously. "Why would we want to do that? I wouldn't want to leave here forever. I have family. We have friends. This is my home. Where would we live?"

I answer, "I don't know. There must be someplace where there aren't any courtrooms."

She laughs. "Every city in the world has courtrooms and I'll be damned if I'll spend the rest of my life on some desert island."

I can see that this conversation is getting us nowhere. "No, I guess that would be out of the question," I say, and then add, "But I wouldn't mind taking off for a year."

As she swims off to do more laps she replies, "That would be wonderful."

I sit there up to my neck in the cooling water, thinking about alternatives, and wonder what I'm going to do. Maybe a year off with Kathy would change how I feel about Elaine. Elaine provides the relief I need from the pressures and stress of my life as a lawyer. But how much does the power of her spell depend upon a willed illusion that I can only be a free spirit with her? Maybe I could escape for a year. Maybe a year off would change my whole perspective.

But I doubt it. I think sadly to myself that I've been doing what I do for over twenty years. I'm not sure that a year off would help me see things more clearly or change my feelings for Elaine. Yes, maybe they're based on a willed illusion. But their power over my will can't be denied. They're like a demon inside me that won't be exorcised. So is Elaine the answer? Am I ready to let myself be possessed completely? I just don't know.

CHAPTER 35

It's Friday morning and I pull my rented car into a vacant parking spot at the Hilo Courthouse. I've tried a number of cases in Hilo but this has been my first in the newly constructed building. The building has two modern circuit courts, both of which are state of the art. The air conditioning and sound system actually work, there are two attorney conference rooms and even a new coffee machine in the jury deliberation room. Entering the courtroom I see the court clerk and Bill Peters.

The clerk looks up and says to me, "I'm glad you're here. The judge wants you and Mr. Peters to see if you can settle before the jury is called in.

We walk into one of the conference rooms and I say to Peters, "Bill, I really think your clients are foolish not to accept $30,000. There's no disputing the fact that the lanai door was covered with decals, the judge has denied all of your proposed instructions concerning the Uniform Building Code and will, in fact, instruct the jury that there was no law in effect requiring shatter proof glass. In addition, the kid admitted on cross examination that after jumping over the railing he ran through the door. I think it's going to be a defense verdict."

Peters looks tired and downcast. "Mark, everything you say is true, but I have very stubborn clients. I can't convince them to take any less than $75,000. Remember they were stuck on $100,000 and it took all my powers of persuasion for them to drop their demand. Can't you convince the carrier to come up to $75,000?"

I shake my head. "Absolutely not. I've spoken to them every day this week and they remain firm at $30,000." Actually, what I'm saying is true. The company refuses to budge.

As Bill leaves the room he says, without much hope in his voice, that he'll try one more time. Closing arguments start in about fifteen minutes so I start reviewing my notes. I'll be glad to get out of Hilo. It's been raining since my arrival; the hotel, a sister hotel of the Kona Beach, is second rate; my room is not only dark but has no desk. The hotel advertises that it's on the bay but looking out my window all I see are some tired looking palm trees and a driveway. Making matters worse my room is directly under a bar where music is played until the early morning hours. I tried to change rooms but the manager insisted that there were no vacancies. I find it difficult to believe that people actually come to Hilo for a vacation.

I re-enter the courtroom and walk to the counsel table. The room is now empty except for Art Ramirez, assistant manager of the Kona Beach Hotel. He's been spending the week with his sister and her family who live in Hilo. Lucky guy, no hotel room for him.

As I sit, he says, "Do you think it'll finish today? I'd love to be home for the weekend."

I reply. "Absolutely. We'll give our summations, the judge will instruct the jury and then you can leave."

"What about you?" He asks.

"I'll stick around for a few hours. Hopefully, the jury won't take too long to reach a verdict." As I say this, Peters walks in with his clients. I look at him but he shakes his head indicating that there's no settlement.

The jury enters and the members sit in their usual places. I look them over feeling pleased. Not one has a teenager, most are in their forties and fifties, only one in her twenties and she has no children. The foreperson will probably be juror number five, a retired accountant. They all have contented looks so I assume they've had a good night's sleep. More than I can say for myself.

Moments later all stand as the judge enters. Everyone likes Judge Hashimoto, a former state senator, probably the most pleasant person I've ever known. He even looks pleasant, resembling Santa Claus with a plump round face and perpetual smile. He's polite and courteous to everyone in his courtroom, especially lawyers. Despite the fact that he's plaintiff oriented, he's never shown the slightest trace of favoritism in any of my trials with him. Though not the smartest judge on the bench, I wish every judge had his temperament and demeanor.

"Good morning, ladies and gentlemen." Judge Hashimoto smiles down at us. "Let the record show that all parties are present with their counsel. We will now commence closing arguments. Mr. Peters, you may proceed."

Peters speaks for about forty five minutes. Most of his time is spent on the injuries suffered by his client and the long term effects he will suffer. He briefly discusses liability as if it were a foregone conclusion that the hotel was negligent. He admits that there were decals on the door but argues that even though there was no legal requirement the hotel should have installed shatter proof glass. As he finishes I can see the female members of the jury looking at Scott with sympathetic eyes.

The judge motions for me to proceed and I talk for about the same length of time, starting by expressing my heartfelt sympathy for the boy, telling the jury how sad we, especially the employees of the hotel, are for his injuries. Then I emphasize some of the instructions the judge will read to the jury - that they can use their common sense, not to allow sympathy to enter into their deliberations, to follow the law as set forth by the court.

I spend the major part of my time on liability. explaining that the Uniform Building Code which was in effect at the time the hotel was built expressly stated the type of glass to be used in sliding glass doors and nothing was mentioned regarding the use of shatter proof glass. I tell them that there was absolutely no evidence presented, thus no proof, that shatter proof glass was even available at the time the hotel was built or that it could have prevented the type of injuries experienced by the plaintiff. I tell them that the hotel acted reasonably in following the Uniform Building Code and that the employees acted in a reasonable manner by the placement of decals on the door. I then argue that the plaintiff was obviously in a rush to answer the phone. I ask, "Do you believe the plaintiff acted in a reasonable manner by jumping over the lanai railing and running into his parents' room without even looking at the door to see whether it was open or not? I suggest that he did not act as a reasonable person would act." I conclude by going over the jury verdict form and suggesting that they find no negligence on the part of the hotel.

Judge Hashimoto reads the jury instructions after which the jury goes out to deliberate. Within an hour they return with a defense verdict. I walk over and shake hands with Peters and his clients, wishing them good luck. Mrs Williams, surprisingly, gives me a hug and whispers in my ear, "I wish we had hired you to represent us." Again, I wish her luck.

I arrive at the airport with an hour to go before my flight home. I walk into the bar, order a beer and take it to a corner booth. Sipping my beer, I think about the Williams, asking myself why I don't feel good about this one.

Chapter 36

The following day Frank, David and I are having lunch at a new Chinese restaurant in Chinatown. Frank has highly recommended it, but I like Sings noodles better. I say to Frank, "The noodles at Sings are better."

"You should've ordered the won ton soup, it's wonderful," he says as he slurps another spoonful into his mouth. "Congratulations again, how was Hilo?"

"Thanks," I reply. "Hilo was wet and boring. What they need are some good restaurants. I ate at Ken's Pancake House every night. Their chicken fried steak isn't bad but it does get old after awhile."

Frank says, "Sounds monotonous to me. But at least the trial went alright."

"The trial went okay but I felt sorry for the kid. I wish they had taken our offer. I think they would've had a better chance of winning if the case had been properly prepared."

David asks, "What do you mean?"

I play with my noodles, "Bill Peters is a nice guy, but from the moment we started jury selection it was obvious that he was inexperienced. He should've hired an expert witness to testify that at the time the hotel was built, even though not required by code, shatter proof glass should have been installed. A reasonable developer of a resort hotel, knowing that children would be on the premises, should have installed shatter proof glass, and, if such glass were installed, the boy wouldn't have experienced such serious injuries."

Frank nods his head in agreement. "It's too bad they don't have a certification requirement for various legal specialties. We handle too many cases against lawyers who aren't qualified to try personal injury cases. The same should hold true for a number of specialties."

"I agree. It doesn't seem right for lawyers to hold themselves out as specialists when they've never even tried a case. Also, if I consult a lawyer who says he specializes in taxation how do I know if he's truly qualified. It's required of doctors and should also be required of lawyers. Hopefully that day will arrive."

Frank adds. "Not as long as bar associations worry more about lawyers than they do about clients."

We finish our lunch and walk back to our office. After a week in Hilo the sun feels good. David and I go to my room and I look at the pile of mail that has accumulated during my absence. I complain to David. "I'll probably have to spend all day tomorrow catching up with all of this. Who's our judge on the escalator case?"

David places the folder on my desk. "Judge Sakumoto. I think the case is ready to go. The only live witnesses in addition to the plaintiff will be representatives from our client, the state inspector and a representative of the manufacturer. Our people will testify as to the gap required by the manufacturer, previous inspections, including one that took place days before the accident, and the inspection immediately following the accident. All inspections establish that the gap was correct. This will be confirmed by the state inspector. The manufacturer's rep will confirm the designated space of the gap."

I ask, "Will there be any live testimony from doctors?"

"No, all doctors have been deposed. There's her knee surgeon, her orthopedic doctor and her family doctor. You've stipulated that the emergency hospital records can be admitted without further foundation."

I say, "Sounds to me like it'll be straightforward. We should easily finish on Friday. Isn't the Morrison case coming up the following Monday?"

David smiles. "You mean the nutcase from Omaha? Julie's been working on that one. But, yes, the escalator case should finish by Friday. Bill Grady is opposing counsel and he's very competent. We went over the depositions together and he knows what he's doing."

"I agree," I say. "He's very experienced and a nice guy on top of it. I'm sure it'll go with no hangups. If Julie is still here please send her in and I'll see you Monday morning. Ask her if she'd bring me a cup of coffee."

Leaning back in my chair, I close my eyes. As always these days, whenever I have a moment to reflect, I think about the decision I have to make. It can't be put off indefinitely. I won't make a decision until the

Morrison case is concluded, but the thought of not doing this any more is becoming more and more appealing. I let myself imagine how it will play out if I follow my inclinations. I think that the house can be sold and Frank can buy my interest in the firm. I'll leave Kathy and we'll divide what we have. There should be more than enough to last for a number of years. Of course, I still have to get my girls through school. I'm sure I can figure something out. What I can't calculate is the human cost. Am I ready to break up a good marriage and inflict terrible pain on a woman I love? Is a new life with Elaine worth what I'll be giving up? Breaking into my reveries is Julie with two huge folders under each arm and a coffee cup in her hand.

Julie hands me the coffee and places the folders on my desk. I can't see the desktop through all of the papers and folders now covering it. I ask Julie to bring me current on the Morrison case.

She begins. "As you may recall, this is the case where the desk clerk mistakenly gave Morrison's room key to some Japanese tourists. When they entered the room Mr. Morrison went bananas."

I smile. "Is the phrase 'bananas' a recognized medical term?"

Julia laughs. "Absolutely! It's used in every psychiatric journal I've ever seen. You took his deposition in Omaha. How did he appear to you?"

I answer, "Like a real fruitcake. Who are the liability witnesses?"

Julie tries to look very serious. "Actually, the correct medical terminology is 'nutcase'. The only witnesses on liability, in addition to the Morrisons, are the desk clerk and the security guard. Both will testify that Morrison came down to the lobby yelling that there was a conspiracy and to call the police. They tried to explain what happened and to calm him down but he kept insisting that it was a conspiracy and to call the police."

"At his deposition Morrison testified that he was taken away by ambulance."

Julie shakes her head. "That's not correct. The emergency room records show he was brought there by taxi. Mrs. Morrison was also trying to calm him down. Then he started complaining about his heart and told the desk clerk to call an ambulance. The clerk was so irritated by him that she told him to call a cab. Mrs. Morrison did and they went outside to wait for it."

I ask, "How does the medical testimony look?"

"He was taken to emergency and given all types of tests and then released. Apparently they could find nothing wrong with his heart. Their attorney has stipulated that the emergency room records can be admitted without calling anyone from the hospital. I stipulated that the records of his family physician and Omaha psychiatrist can be admitted without further foundation."

I nod my head. "Good. Neither found anything wrong with him. What about the psychiatrist from Meningers Clinic? He testified that Morrison was suffering from post traumatic stress syndrome. I've had a number of cases involving post traumatic stress syndrome and most of them were legitimate and quite serious. I realize that Meningers is very highly respected, but to say that Morrison has PTSS from this incident seems like a lot of crap to me."

Julie frowns. "That may be true for a normal person but according to our psychiatrist, Dr. Bertram, Morrison had some serious pre-existing mental problems. He still carried emotional scars from his days as a prisoner in a Japanese prisoner of war camp and the stress of his business was causing him some severe problems. He's the classic egg shell plaintiff."

It's my turn to frown. "So we have to take the plaintiff as we find him. Does that mean we're responsible for all of his existing mental problems?"

Julie answers. "That's right. And his problems are very significant. Even Dr. Bertram confirms that his present psychological difficulties are quite substantial. As a matter of fact he's almost non-functional."

Julie and I spend some time reviewing all of the medical testimony. I look at my watch and see that it's after four. I send her home and continue to sit at my desk staring out the window. I'm constantly amazed at the ever changing skyline which is now covered by a multitude of high rises.

I pick up the phone and dial Elaine. She answers. "Hello."

I say, "Hi, it's me. How are you?"

"I'm okay. You sound tired."

I'm exhausted. I was in trial all week and at work all day."

She sighs. "You poor thing. When am I going to see you?"

I lean back. "I'll be in trial this week and I have another one starting next week. Hopefully, after that. What are you doing?"

She laughs. "We just finished dinner and I sent the kids to watch TV while I clean up. We're all going to watch a movie so I'll make some popcorn. A typical exciting Saturday night."

I laugh. "If I can ever get out of here it'll be the same for me. That is, if I can keep my eyes open."

We chat for a few more minutes and say goodbye. I close my eyes and think of Kathy. She picked me up at the airport last night and we went to the Outrigger Club for dinner. The night was beautiful as was Kathy. We had a wonderful meal under the stars overlooking the ocean. What could be more perfect? Sometimes I think I must be as nutty as poor Mr. Morrison. Can I really be thinking of giving up this woman? I close my eyes and doze off.

The ringing of my private line wakes me out of a deep sleep. My watch tells me it's almost five, meaning I'd slept for almost an hour. It's Kathy wanting to know when I'll be home. Telling her I'm about ready to leave, she asks, "What do you want for dinner?"

"If you take out a couple of steaks," I tell her, "I'll grill them when I get home." She tells me she'll have a nice cold martini waiting for me and we say goodbye.

Leaning back, I start thinking about the Morrison case. Something just doesn't seem right. It's difficult to believe that the hotel should be responsible for all of his problems as a result of such an innocuous incident. I can understand being momentarily startled, but to go off the deep end. It just doesn't feel right.

I walk down to our conference room. A comfortable room, it contains a large koa wood table surrounded by eight chairs. It also doubles as our library with shelves that contain the Hawaii Revised Statutes, the Hawaiian Supreme Court Reports as well as a reasonable number of miscellaneous books on specific subjects. It's certainly not comprehensive enough for serious legal research but the Supreme Court library is only a few blocks away and is excellent. I look through several digests to see if I can find something, but my research skills are almost non-existent. I guess that comes from relying too much on associates. I decide to leave the research to Julie. As I take the elevator down to the parking garage I can almost feel the taste of an ice cold martini and the aroma of steaks broiling on the grill.

CHAPTER 37

Once again I'm in Frank's office sipping some unidentifiable liqueur while watching Frank blow smoke rings with the largest cigar I've ever seem. It must be Cuban. I ask him about the liqueur. I don't want to hear about the cigar.

Frank leans back in what must be the most expensive executive chair in Hawaii and tells me, "Yesterday afternoon the jury returned a defense verdict in the 'eye-out' case."

"Was that the one where the plaintiff lost his eye when the cork came flying out of the champagne bottle?" I ask. "I never did understand what his theory was. Don't champagne corks do that?"

Frank nods. "Correct on both counts. We represented the distributor who brought the champagne in from California. The plaintiff also sued the producer and the retailer. His complaint against the producer was that the bottles didn't have adequate warnings on their labels."

I say, "It seems to me that everyone knows what happens when you open a bottle of champagne. But what was his theory against the distributor?"

"You're right. Everyone does know. He claimed the distributor allowed the bottles to get too shook up in transit."

I can't help but laugh. "Did he think the distributor had the power to smooth out the Pacific Ocean?"

Frank is also laughing. "That's exactly what I asked the jury. It was a defense verdict for each of the defendants. The distributor was so pleased he sent me a bottle of this very extraordinary and, undoubtedly, very expensive liqueur." He takes another sip and blows another smoke ring. "Enjoy!"

A Reasonable Person

I also take another sip. "It does taste good but it's definitely unusual. What do you have for Monday?"

Frank looks me in the eye and asks in a grave tone, "How should I know. It's only Friday."

I feel my heart skip a beat but Frank grins. "Gotcha!"

I slump in my chair. "How about a vodka on the rocks? You're absolutely turning me into an alcoholic."

He's still grinning. "Sorry about that. I have one on Kauai. It involves a car accident. It's ready to go. Laurie did most of the prep."

I ask, "How is she working out. She seems very competent."

Frank responds enthusiastically, "She's excellent. Smart as a whip and a hard worker. She's been a great help. How did your escalator case go?"

I take another sip which empties my glass and hold it out for a refill. "We argued this morning and the jury came back an hour ago with a defense verdict."

Frank asks, "Did Bill Grady represent the plaintiff?"

I answer. "Yes, and he did a good job but it was a weak case against the maintenance company. There was no dispute about the fact that they completely complied with the manufacturers' specifications."

"Did the jury find the manufacturer liable?"

I shake my head. "Bill settled with the manufacturer before the trial started. They didn't pay too much. Naturally, I argued that if anyone was to blame it was the manufacturer."

"What did Bill argue?"

"He really didn't have much to argue about as far as the actual maintenance was concerned, but he did come up with an ingenious idea. He argued that yellow lines should have been painted along the sides of the steps as a warning not to stand too close to the railing."

Frank smiles. "Clever, but wouldn't that apply more to the manufacturer than to the maintenance company?"

I nod. "That's exactly what I told the jury. I also pointed out there was no evidence that yellow lines would have prevented this particular accident. I still think the real cause was the cake that was dropped at the bottom."

As Frank pours another glass of the liqueur, Laurie enters the room. Frank tells her to sit and asks if she wants a glass. She says she does and as he pours for her, he says, "I agree and apparently the jury did too. Do you have one starting next week?"

Laurie has been quietly sipping her drink but now asks me, "Don't you have the case involving the guy from Omaha? Julie was telling me about it. Isn't he suing for serious mental distress?"

I look at her. She's not only smart but very attractive with light auburn hair and clear hazel eyes. She was of invaluable assistance to me in the declaratory relief action involving the bat wielding restaurant owner. Her research was very helpful in obtaining a decision in our favor. I answer her. "That's right. Ever since the incident at the hotel his main activity is sitting on his front porch and staring at the horizon."

Laurie says, "According to Julie, he was pretty screwed up before the incident."

"Yes," I reply, but he was functioning and we have to take the plaintiff as we find him."

Frank interjects, "He sounds to me like the classical egg shell plaintiff."

"Are you familiar with the flood case that was decided about ten years ago by the Hawaii Supreme Court?" Laurie's directing her question to me.

I'm finding it difficult taking my eyes away from her legs. They're absolutely lovely. "I am," I finally answer. "It held that a plaintiff can recover for serious mental distress even though there was no physical injury."

Laurie pulls her skirt down a few inches and nods, "That's right. We studied it in our law school torts class. The State of Hawaii was sued for a flooding that destroyed the plaintiffs' house. The plaintiffs not only sued for the loss of their home but also for serious mental distress. It was the first case in the United States where recovery for mental distress was allowed even though there was no physical injury."

I now look into her bright, intense eyes and ask, "How does that help us?"

She smiles. "Let me get the case. I'll be right back."

She leaves the room and Frank says, "Have you noticed her legs? They're great." Then he adds, "She must have something going on in that pretty little head of hers."

I say, "I only hope that it's nothing that belongs to you."

Frank laughs, "No way! She's a happily married woman."

I think to myself that this wouldn't be the first time Frank has become involved with a married woman, but he does look sincere and this time I actually believe him.

Laurie re-enters the room with what appears to be a volume of the Hawaii Supreme Court Reports. She opens it, finds the page she's looking for and reads. "Serious mental distress may be found where a reasonable man, normally constituted, would be unable to adequately cope with the mental stress engendered by the circumstances of the case."

She continues. "Thus, for a jury to find serious mental distress in a case involving no physical injury the plaintiff must be a reasonable person, normally constituted. From what Julie told me, Mr. Morrison had a myriad of prior mental problems." She puts down the book and takes a large swallow of her drink.

I say, "The question is whether a reasonable person, normally constituted would be able to adequately cope with the mental distress engendered by the circumstances of this case. I've always felt that a normal person would not have had such a serious reaction."

Frank says. "Not a 'normal' person. There's no such thing in the law. It's a 'reasonable' person."

I argue, "A 'reasonable' person, 'normally' constituted. Isn't that the same as a normal person?"

"I don't know." Frank and Laurie blurt out at the same time. Then Laurie says, "I'll do some research on that tomorrow."

Laurie puts her glass down and gets up to leave. "Thanks," I tell her. "I already feel better about the case." As she walks out, I add, "Please close the door."

Frank re-fills his glass with the liqueur, holds out the bottle and asks, "Do you want some more?"

"No, thanks," I reply, but I would like to talk to you alone for a moment.

"What's up?" He asks.

"We're worried about you." I tell him. "I'm worried about you. Is there something going on that you're not telling us?"

Frank looks at me, puts down his glass, and says, "Yes, there is. Did you know that Donna re-married?"

Donna was his first wife. I nod, "Yes, but I've never met her new husband."

Frank continues. "He's a nice guy, but his company is transferring him to Cleveland."

I ask, "What about your kids?"

"That's the problem," he replies. "They're all going to go." His eyes are beginning to tear.

"Have you spoken to a lawyer about this?" I ask.

Tears are running freely down his face, "I've talked with two, and they both say the same thing, there's nothing I can do. They want to be with their mother. I can fly them back for a period of time during the summer and, perhaps, alternate holidays, but I can't prevent them from going."

I don't know what to say, he's been a devoted father and cares deeply for his children. I also realize that he brought most of this on himself. Donna spent many of her lonely hours crying on Kathy's shoulder during the final stage of their marriage. Finally, I respond, "I know how you feel, I miss my girls."

Frank looks at me, reading my mind as usual, "I admit Donna had good reason to leave me, but that's not the point. At least, you were with your girls while they were growing up. I'm going to miss out on that. It's just not fair." He's openly crying now. He then adds, "Something must really be wrong with me, I can't even keep a girlfriend anymore."

He wipes his tears and we sit quietly for a few minutes. "Frank, you know if there's anything I can do for you all you have to do is ask."

He smiles through his tears. "I know that, but you have your own problems, your own decisions." He spreads his arms, "I'm getting to feel more and more like you. I'm getting sick and tired of all this." He seems to be encompassing everything.

I look at him seriously, "Maybe you should speak with Dr. Bertram. He's very impressive."

He laughs, "You think I need a shrink?"

"I don't think it can hurt," I reply. "By the way, I checked my calendar and I have no trials for two weeks following next week's trial. They've all settled. We can spend some time together."

Frank says, "Thanks, Mark. I know I can always count on you, and I'll be behind you no matter what decision you make. But, as I told you before, I think you'd be making a huge mistake if you leave Kathy. Naturally I hate to see you put our firm in jeopardy, but whatever you decide to do, I'll be your friend. I'm always behind you."

We shake hands and I leave. As I drive home I think of his parting words. Can he really mean what he said? Of course he'll try to be supportive, but he must see putting the firm in jeopardy as a betrayal. Am I really ready to betray my best friend and leave my wife? Is Elaine worth it?

CHAPTER 38

The weekend passes quickly and I'm now sitting in Judge Shea's courtroom next to the general manager of the Queen Hotel, Jim Harrison. Though he knows almost nothing of the case, he volunteered to sit with me at the trial. I couldn't be more pleased. He's one of the most impressive Hawaiian men I've ever met, tall and dark with almost Hollywood like features, thick grayish hair and a warm smile that can't help but impact every female that's fortunate enough to be selected for this jury.

At the plaintiff's table are the Morrisons with their attorney, James Bradshaw. I've never tried a case against him but according to attorneys I've asked, Bradshaw is very smart and a competent trial lawyer. He's in his mid-forties, about six feet, somewhat slender and pleasant looking, wearing a well tailored charcoal gray suit. He looks like a tough opponent. I should have listened to Kathy and bought a new suit when we were in Chicago.

Behind us, seated in the gallery, is the jury panel. On Saturday six of us had lunch at Sings and discussed the type of juror I should look for. David suggested young men, as they wouldn't tend to identify with the plaintiffs. Julie agreed but suggested I wouldn't want anyone who had a close relative or friend with mental problems. Both Laurie and Sidney also agreed but added that they wouldn't want men or women in their late forties or early fifties. Frank seemed distracted and when I repeated the question to him, he replied. "I wouldn't want any nut cases on the jury." The table was immediately silenced and I thought that once this trial is over I'll again suggest that Frank see Dr. Bertram. However, looking over the potential jurors I think I owe Frank an apology. He was the only one who was absolutely right. The jury will have to determine whether, prior to the hotel incident, the plaintiff was a reasonable person, normally constituted. Whether young or old, men or women, I want twelve reasonable people on the jury. All nut cases will be excused. Of course, recognizing a nutcase can be difficult, but, I intend to excuse anyone who responds strangely to my questioning.

At this moment the Bailiff directs everyone to stand and Judge William Shea enters. This is one of his first civil trials and my first with him. In his early fifties, a former city prosecutor, he's been on the bench for about five years, hearing mainly criminal cases. He has a reputation for being knowledgeable and fair and for having a good judicial temperament.

He sits and scans the courtroom thoughtfully and with wise looking eyes. "May the record show," he announces, "the presence of the plaintiffs and their counsel and the presence of defendant by its representative and its counsel. Please be seated. Counsels, are you ready to proceed?"

We both rise and answer in the affirmative. I wonder whether this will be my last trial in the State of Hawaii, but I can't think about that now. I need to focus on this case.

Judge Shea then directs his remarks to the jury panel. "The clerk will now pick twelve of your names at random. As your name is called please take a seat in the jury box."

The clerk picks a card from the box in front of him and calls out, "Alice Garcia." A dark, pleasant looking, middle aged woman rises and walks self consciously to the jury box. Jury selection has begun.

. . .

It's now 7:30AM on Friday morning and Frank and I are in our coffee room. Frank fills both of our cups with hot steaming coffee. I take a bite of my strudel and say, "Welcome home. How was Kauai?"

"You know how these neighbor island trials are," he replies. We're in court all day, have a quiet dinner alone and then back to the hotel to prepare for the following day. Not too much fun."

I grimace. "You're absolutely right. That's exactly how it is. How did your trial go?" I know nothing about the case.

"The trial went fine," he says without his usual enthusiasm. "Our client was one of the sugar companies. They were burning their sugar cane preparatory to its harvesting."

"It was one of those smoke on the road cases," I guess. "Don't tell me, the driver ignored the warnings and drove into the smoke?"

"Absolutely right," Frank laughs. "Usually it's a tourist, but in this case it was a long time resident who should've known better. There were flags and two signal men trying to caution her to slow down but she was late for work and sped into the smoke. Her car ended up over fifty yards into the cane field after having flown over an eight foot ditch."

"She was really flying. What was the result?" I ask.

Frank shrugs. "Before final argument he reduced his demand from $100,000 to $5,000. I called the carrier and they said to settle. We ended up settling for $3,500."

"That's a great result," I say. You should be very pleased."

Again, he shrugs. "I returned last night to a lonely apartment, had a glass of wine and went to bed. There's no pleasure having no one to share it with. Have you finished your trial yet?"

Though his demeanor and tone concern and sadden me, I don't know how to cheer him up, so I just reply, "Both sides have rested and closing arguments start in an hour."

Two of our secretaries enter the coffee room chattering about their weekend plans. Frank and I refill our cups and go to my office. Frank sits on my couch and asks, "How's the jury?"

"I like them," I reply. "I took your advice and tried to exclude all nut cases. I not only listened to their answers, but paid even more attention to their manner of answering, their demeanor, their expressions and their conduct. I think we ended up with twelve reasonable people."

Frank smiles. "Good, that's what I was trying to tell you. How did the testimony go?"

"I think it went well," I answer. "Bradshaw wasn't aware of the flood case and was basing his entire case on the 'eggshell man' theory. On cross-examination the sons admitted that Morrison was barely functioning before the hotel incident. They testified that the business had passed him by and that he would sit in his office doing basically nothing for hours at a time. They said that any advice he tried to give them was absolutely wrong. Bradshaw never objected to any of their testimony."

"So," Frank says, "it was shown that he was not a reasonable person before the accident?"

"I think so," I say. "It got even better. Mrs. Morrison testified that her husband was so depressed before the incident that their friends didn't want to be around him. She thought the trip to Hawaii would help but even before the intrusion he was acting strangely and withdrawing into himself. She described the incident as being the final straw. Again, no objection."

"How was Morrison?" Frank inquires.

"Even stranger than at his deposition," I answer. He claimed that he didn't even know his street address. It would take him at least a minute to try to answer the simplest of questions. He was like someone from outer space. He was on the stand for at least four hours."

Frank then asks, "What about his POW experience? Did you ask him about that?"

"Yes," I respond. "He said it was a very frightening experience. He said that guards would come in the middle of the night and take away one of the American prisoners who would never be seen again. It sounded awful to me. When the Asian men entered his room at the hotel he felt like he was taken back in time."

"Did Dr. Bertram testify?" Frank asks.

"Yes, he was very good. He basically confirmed that Morrison was barely functioning prior to the hotel incident and that, in his opinion, it would take very little, if anything, to push him over the edge. If Bradshaw's eggshell theory had held up, the jury could come back with millions. But, yesterday afternoon, Judge Shea approved our instructions based on the flood case."

"How did Bradshaw take it?" Frank asks.

"He turned pale," I answer. "I almost felt sorry for him. He saw his entire case going down the tubes." I look at my watch and rise. "Time to go, see you later."

Frank wishes me good luck as I head out the door.

CHAPTER 39

There's five minutes to spare as I enter the courtroom. Everyone appears to be in their correct positions. I sit at the counsel table next to Harrison and pull out my notes for my closing argument. Turning to Jim, I ask, "What do you think?"

He smiles, "I've really enjoyed this. I think you've both done a good job. I'm looking forward to listening to closing arguments."

He's interrupted by the entry of the judge. After the usual preliminaries, Judge Shea says, "We will now hear summations. Mr. Bradford, you may begin."

Bradford stands and places his notes on the podium. He's wearing a beautifully tailored dark blue suit with a solid maroon tie. His voice is deep and soft. He tells the jury the story of his client, how Morrison joined the marines as a youngster and was taken prisoner, how after the war he went to work for an oil company as a mechanic and ended up owning the division he had once worked for.

He then says, "It's true that before the hotel incident he had some problems, but he was functioning productively and was president of the company. Let's go to the night of the event. He and his wife were soundly sleeping, feeling secure in the safety of their hotel room. Suddenly in the early hours of the morning he's shocked, awakened by his wife's screaming and three intruders. He looks at his wife's bed and can't see her. Can you imagine how upset and traumatized he must have been, how frightening an experience like that can be. I suggest that any reasonable person would have the same reaction."

He tells the jury that since the incident Morrison has been non-functional, that he's basically lost his business, lost his friends, lost everything that is important to a man.

"In conclusion," he says, "I suggest that we've proven by a preponderance of the evidence that the hotel was negligent, that no matter how busy or harassed the clerk was she should not have given out the wrong key. We have proven that as a result of the hotel's negligence the plaintiff sustained serious mental distress and I suggest that for Mr. Morrison to be fully and fairly compensated, that you should bring back a verdict of no less than $2,000,000. Thank you very much."

I turn to Harrison and say, "What do you think now?"

"I just hope we have enough insurance," he replies.

Judge Shea motions for me to proceed and I step up to the lectern. I begin by telling the jury that in order to find in favor of the plaintiff that he must prove every aspect of his case by a preponderance of the evidence. I tell them how much we all sympathize with the plaintiff, but the court will instruct them that they should not allow sympathy for either side to enter into their deliberations. I tell them that they can and should use their common sense in helping them arrive at a decision.

"Ladies and gentlemen," I then say, "You are the finders of fact but you are duty bound to follow the law as instructed by the court. Whether we like the law or not we have been sworn to follow it."

"As you know," I continue, "The plaintiff is claiming serious mental distress. The court will instruct you that, in the absence of physical injury, serious mental distress may be found where a reasonable man, normally constituted would be unable to adequately cope with the mental stress engendered by the circumstances of the case."

I tell them that in this case there was no physical injury, that no one touched him. "Even his own emergency room records," I say, "show that he was not physically injured. They examined him, concluded that there was no heart attack or other injuries and released him."

"Thus," I continue, "You must determine whether before the hotel incident the plaintiff was a reasonable person, normally constituted and, if so, whether that man, that reasonable man, would be unable to cope with the mental stress engendered by the incident which took place at the hotel."

I then review the testimony emphasizing the factors which indicated he was far from being a reasonable person before the incident. I read them portions of the sons' testimony in which they both agreed that he would sit in his office for hours; if asked for a decision it was invariably wrong, that he was incapable of running the business. I remind them of Mrs. Morrison's testimony stating that he was withdrawing into himself and was losing all of his friends due to his increasingly depressive moods. I point out his experiences as a prisoner and how frightened he'd be when the guards entered their barracks in the middle of the night. "Thus," I conclude, "He certainly was not a reasonable person, normally constituted before this incident occurred."

"But," I continue, "That's not really the test. The question is not how the plaintiff reacted but what effect the incident would have on a reasonable person, normally constituted. Let me give you an example. Let's suppose that you are sitting in your car and are suddenly and without warning struck from the rear, causing immediate and sharp pain in your neck or back. As a result you can't work, you lose your job, are unable to help support your family and have to undergo lengthy medical treatment. As a further result of your physical injury you suffer serious mental distress, become very depressed, need psychiatric or psychological help. For this type of situation there is no 'reasonable man' test. Your serious mental distress arose out of a physical injury and even if you were barely functional, as the plaintiff was before the incident, the person who struck you would be responsible for all of your present problems, physical and mental."

I pause, look around the courtroom and see that the gallery is full. I see David, Julie, Sidney and Laurie, as well as a number of other attorneys. I turn back to the jury, and say, "However, Let's change that scenario a little. Let's suppose that while driving you are momentarily distracted, look ahead and see that a car has suddenly stopped in front of you. You immediately slam on your brakes and your car comes to a loud screeching stop with only inches to spare between the two cars. The person in the car ahead of you is, of course, startled and maybe even scared. He takes your license number and leaves. One year later you are served with a lawsuit in which that person is claiming serious mental distress. He's suing you for thousands of dollars in psychiatric bills and lost time from work due to his being so frightened by your actions."

I can see that all of the jurors are smiling and shaking their heads. I continue, "The test is not whether that driver suffered serious mental distress but whether such an incident would have caused serious mental distress in a reasonable man, normally constituted. Obviously it would not. The same holds true for the hotel incident. Certainly a reasonable person would be startled, even momentarily frightened, but certainly not to the extreme state that the plaintiff is now claiming. A good example of that is Mrs. Morrison. She was also scared but within minutes was trying to get her husband to calm down and otherwise was perfectly fine. Those are the reactions of a reasonable person. Now the jurors are nodding in agreement. A very good sign.

"In conclusion, ladies and gentlemen," I say, "The first question on the jury verdict form is, 'Was defendant's negligence the cause of plaintiff's claim for serious mental distress?' I suggest that the answer is 'No.' First, there was no negligence. I agree that the desk clerk made a little mistake but under the circumstances it was certainly just that, a little mistake. Of more importance is that if you find the hotel was negligent certainly that was not the cause of the mental distress claimed by the plaintiff. If your answer is 'No' you need go no further on the verdict form, just have the foreperson sign and date it. Thank you very much for your attention."

I sit and Harrison whispers, "With you on our side we don't need insurance. Thank you very much."

The judge motions for Bradford to deliver his rebuttal. He stands and says, "Your honor, the plaintiff will waive rebuttal."

I'm amazed. Even Judge Shea looks surprised as he blurts out, "Are you certain?"

"Yes, your honor." Bradford sits.

I find this hard to believe. I've never seen this happen before. Judge Shea says, "In that case I will now instruct the jury."

The jury is instructed and taken to lunch before they start deliberating. I shake hands with Harrison who again thanks me before leaving. I think that he's the first client to thank me since Mrs. Lee a few years before. I don't count Mrs. Thomas, the ex-hooker, who invited me to her home so she could thank me "properly" after obtaining a directed verdict in her favor the year before.

Bradshaw walks over and shakes hands before leaving with his clients. The only ones remaining in the courtroom are my associates who each walk over and shake hands with me. David is the first to speak. "Little mistake? Where did that come from?"

I shake my head. "I thought the jury was with me," I reply, "so I thought I'd push it a little." I realize that wasn't the brightest thing to say.

Laurie asks. "Is it common to waive rebuttal?"

David speaks up. "Absolutely not. I've never seen that happen before."

"Neither have I," I say, "As far as I'm concerned that's the same as giving up." I then say, "Why don't we all go to lunch. I can use some noodles and we can talk about it there.

We return to court later that afternoon. Bradshaw is there with Mrs. Morrison. Neither Mr. Morrison or his sons are present. The foreperson announces that the jury has reached a decision. Mrs. Garcia hands the verdict form to the clerk who hands it to the judge. Judge Shea reads it, hands it back to the clerk who reads, "Was defendant's negligence the cause of plaintiff's claim for serious mental distress? Answer, 'No.' Dated and signed by Alice Garcia, Foreperson."

I sit back and think that now it's time to fish or cut bait.

CHAPTER 40

It's early Monday morning and dark enough on the freeway for me to turn on my headlights. I pull into our parking garage and see Frank's Porsche parked in its designated space. I park next to it surprised that Frank is in so early. Perhaps living alone is changing his work habits.

Getting off the elevator on the first level, I walk to Freida's. She's opening her door and I enter with a greeting, "Good morning Freida. Have you seen Frank?"

She shakes her head. "No, but I just opened for business. As usual, you're my first customer."

Buying two strudels, I take the elevator to our floor. The front door of our office is unlocked and inside the lights are on. I take the strudels to Frank's office and knock on the closed door. There's no answer.

I open the door and am frozen in shock. Frank is sitting behind his desk, holding a handgun, the back of his head is blown off, pieces of flesh and brain are on the wall behind him. His chair and the wall are covered with blood.

The strudels fall out of my hand and I rush for the bathroom. I reach a commode just in time to throw up. I can't stop heaving for what seems like minutes until gasping for breath I make my way to a sink where I rinse my mouth with hot water. Almost stumbling to my office, I call 911 and the police and coroner soon arrive. Two detectives question me while the coroner and a forensics man are going over the scene in Frank's office. I answer their questions mechanically, without any reflection. My thoughts are focused entirely on Frank. It's so terribly sad. If only I'd tried a little harder to help him deal with his depression. He needed people, and he had no one but me. His kids were being taken from him, and he couldn't maintain a relationship with anyone. His pain, the pain of loneliness, is over, but he's left me with the pain of remembering and thinking about how I might have prevented him from doing it.

As soon as the police are through questioning all of us, I send everyone home for the day. Somehow I manage to drive home.

It's now noon and Kathy and I are sitting on our lanai holding hands without finding it necessary to speak. On a table in front of us are two egg salad sandwiches that neither of us has touched. My tear filled eyes make everything around me seem blurry and colorless. I'm completely listless, even the slightest movement takes all of my effort.

"Is there anything I can get you," Kathy asks, "beer, soda, water?"

"No thanks," I reply. "I should've seen it coming. I should've done something." I keep repeating.

Kathy squeezes my hand. "Stop blaming yourself. You said the police told you he left a note saying he couldn't take it any more. You shouldn't feel guilty."

"I can't help it," I say. I was his best friend, maybe his only real friend, and I feel I wasn't there for him when he really needed me."

"You were always there for him. No one could've prevented this. You have nothing to feel guilty about," she repeats.

I realize that she's probably right, but as tears roll down my cheeks and I gaze at the ocean I continue to wonder if that's really true, if there was anything I could've done.

The following morning, after a sleepless night, I'm again sitting with Kathy on our lanai. She's on the phone telling her supervisor that she won't be in for the day.

"Thank you," I tell her. I don't know what I'd do without you."

"You know I'll always be here for you," she smiles and says. "You can't get rid of me."

I lean over and give her a kiss. She is a gem. Frank's words come back to me. I wasn't willing to listen when he spoke them, but now I see how right he was, and I wonder how I could ever have devalued this gem I married. Poor Frank. He said he would support me in whatever decision I made, and he must have anticipated that I probably was going to make the wrong decision he'd made repeatedly. I owe him a lot.

Picking up the phone, I dial my office and ask for Marsha. After she answers, I tell her, "Tell Ellen to let the staff know that the office will close at noon today, but I want to see her in my office tomorrow morning at nine.

Then I want to meet with our entire staff in the conference room at ten." We say a tearful goodbye. I have some serious thinking to do.

It's early Wednesday morning as I open our office door. My eyes again tear up on seeing the 'Dorsey & Cooper' sign. I glance over at Frank's office and see yellow tape covering the door.

At nine sharp, Ellen enters my office carrying a legal pad and a pen. She's wearing black pants and a long sleeved black top. I stand and we give each other a tight hug. I can see that even this tough Korean lady has been crying. "I'm so sorry," she says. "We're all going to miss him."

"Yes, we will," I agree. "He was a real dynamo."

She sits and says, "Yes, he was a good man. What are your plans? What do you want us to do?"

"There are a number of things to be done," I tell her. "First, there's his office. Find out when the crime scene tape can be removed. I want his office completely cleaned and re-painted. Have his chair cleaned and get rid of it. Buy a new chair."

"What should I do with it?" she asks.

"Give it to Goodwill," I say. "As soon as that's taken care of David can move into that room. Next, order a new sign for the door, 'Dorsey, Hunter & Chung.' Also, order new stationery."

She smiles and says, "David and Julie will be your new partners?"

"Yes," I reply. "I haven't had a chance to talk to them about it, so please don't say anything yet."

Ellen is taking notes. "What else?" she asks.

"Contact our accountant," I reply. "She has to determine the value of Frank's interest in the firm. We'll have to pay that to his estate. You'll have to dig out our partnership agreement. It has a formula which includes his share of the assets, accounts receivable and unbilled hours that the accountant will have to follow."

Ellen's busy writing and I continue. "Finally, we're going to have to add at least six new associates."

Ellen gasps, "Where are we going to put them?" Then adds, "And their secretarial help?"

"We have an option to lease the rest of this floor," I reply. "Tell the building manager that we'll exercise our option and for them to prepare the lease. Dig out all resumes we've received in the last few months. Start calling them in for interviews. If I'm not here, David or Julie can talk to them."

"Anything else?" she asks.

A Reasonable Person

"Not right now," I answer. I look at my watch. "Is everyone going to be in the conference room?"

"Yes," she replies.

I stand and we give each other another hug before she leaves.

Our entire staff has now crowded into our conference room. All of the women are dressed in black, which is in sharp contrast to the brightly colored aloha shirts worn by the men. Standing at the head of the table, I look around and it's clear that most of the women have been crying.

I start by saying to them, "We all realize that what's happened is a terrible tragedy. We all thought the world of Frank and we're going to miss him. However, I want you all to know that this firm will not only survive but will grow. Our client base is solid and we'll continue to get new work. None of you have to be concerned about your jobs. We need you more than ever." I see looks of relief on most of their faces.

I continue. "Frank's parents came in late Monday night. I spoke to them last night and they've made arrangements to have Frank interred at Punchbowl Memorial Cemetery. Services will be on Saturday afternoon. Naturally you are all invited to be there." Kathy and I are having dinner with the Coopers tonight, an event I'm not looking forward to. They're nice people but I'm sure they'll have many questions, questions for which I have no answers.

"In closing," I say, "I think we should all take a moment and say our own private prayers and then have a minute of silence in Frank's memory." Everyone bows their heads and there are several minutes of complete silence in the room.

When they look up, I tell them, "One more thing. If anyone asks you what happened, please tell them that you don't know. First, we don't want it spread around and, second, it's no one's business. Will David and Julie please remain, the rest can go back to what you were doing. Thank you all very much. They leave and my two associates sit.

"The reason I asked you to stay," I tell them, "is to ask you, if you're agreeable, to continue with the firm as partners." Both of their faces break out in huge grins. They rise and Julie gives me a big hug. David shakes my hand and they sit.

"I take it that's a yes?" I ask.

"Absolutely," they both exclaim.

"I have a number of ideas," I tell them, "but, basically, David and I will handle the more serious or complex cases and the others, such as whiplash and slip and falls, will be handled through settlement or trial by Laurie or

Sidney. The four of you should go through our entire caseload and divide them up. We can all meet on Saturday morning and go over the details. Are there any questions?"

David asks, "What about the insurance carriers? Will they agree to this?"

"Yes," I reply, "as long as we show them good results, and I'm sure we will. I spoke to Granger last night and to Ventura this morning. They're both agreeable. In fact, Ventura said he had two new cases to send over. Besides, you're now partners. I'm certain Laurie and Sidney will do well and will be partners in the near future."

Julie, somewhat plaintively asks, "What about me? What are my responsibilities?"

I answer, "You have the toughest job of all. You'll be in charge of all coverage questions and disputes, all difficult legal briefs and all appellate briefs. When you need more help, let us know." Her smile returns.

"You have a lot to do in the next few days so I'll let you go. But there's one more thing. I also had a call this morning from Global Insurance, owner of First Hawaiian. They write the vast majority of lawyers malpractice insurance in Hawaii and want us to do all of their defense work. He said he'd be sending us our first case, a $5,000,000 claim against a major local law firm over a botched property deal."

"Wow!" David blurts out, "That's a major breakthrough."

"Absolutely," I respond. "So, why don't we get back to work?"

I head for the coffee room. I already feel like a big load has been taken off my shoulders. I enter the empty room and pour a cup of what appears to be freshly made coffee. Without Frank there to entertain us, the room seems strangely silent. I go to my office and take a sip of the hot coffee. It has a bitter taste and I set it down on my desk.

I pick up the phone and call Kathy. She answers, "Hello."

"Hi, It's me," I say.

"Hi, sweetie," she says, "What's happening?"

"I was wondering," I respond, "whether it would be possible for you to take off next week?"

"I think so," she says. "I have plenty of unused sick time. But, why?"

"Frank's services are Saturday afternoon." I reply. "I thought we could get away on Sunday for the week."

She laughs. "Where to?"

"What about Paris?" I ask.

A Reasonable Person

She's silent for a few moments, then gasps, "Are you serious? I'd love to go to Paris with you."

"I'll call our travel agent and have her set it up."

She laughs, "I'll pack tonight. I love you."

"I love you too. Bye." We hang up. I call Ellen and ask her to call our travel agent to make the necessary arrangements.

Then I call Bob Crown. "Hi, Bob, this is Mark Dorsey."

"Hi Mark. I just heard the news about Frank. I'm really sorry. You know that we all thought the world of him. What a tragedy, he was so young."

"Thank you," I quickly change the subject and ask, "What are you doing?"

"Same as you," he answers. "Trying to think up some new ways to screw an insurance company."

I laugh, "You're right, I guess we all do feed from the same trough. You free for golf this afternoon?"

He also laughs. "That's the best offer I've had all day. Meet me at the club in thirty minutes. I'll treat for lunch then win it back on the course."

I smile and say, "Not with my handicap you won't. See you in thirty minutes." We hang up and I take another sip of the now cold but still bitter coffee.

I pick up the phone and lean back in my chair. I have one more call to make, Elaine. It's about time I say no to her. It's about time I start acting like a reasonable person.

THE END